Married to
an Opposite

MARRIED TO AN OPPOSITE

Making Personality Differences Work for You

Ron Shackelford

Psychology, Religion, and Spirituality
J. Harold Ellens, Series Editor

Westport, Connecticut
London

Library of Congress Cataloging-in-Publication Data

Shackelford, Ron, 1944–
    Married to an opposite : making personality differences work for you / Ron Shackelford.
       p. cm.—(Psychology, Religion, and Spirituality series)
    Includes bibliographical references and index.
    ISBN 0–275–98161–4 (alk. paper)
    1. Marriage—Psychological aspects. 2. Marital conflict. 3. Personality. 4. Empathy. 5.
Emotional intelligence. 6. Married people—Psychology. 7. Couples—Psychology. I. Title.
HQ728.S45 2003
306.81—dc21   2003053630

British Library Cataloguing in Publication Data is available.

Library of Congress Catalog Card Number: 2003053630
ISBN: 0–275–98161–4

First published in 2003

Praeger Publishers, 88 Post Road West, Westport, CT 06881
An imprint of Greenwood Publishing Group, Inc.
www.praeger.com

Printed in the United States of America

The paper used in this book complies with the
Permanent Paper Standard issued by the National
Information Standards Organization (Z39.48–1984).

10 9 8 7 6 5 4 3 2 1

Dedicated to:

my parents, Ray and Louise,
who over the years have modeled self-giving love at
its most profound level of selflessness,

my son, Tobin, and daughter, Tamara,
who patiently tolerated their dad's late nights at
the computer keyboard—apart from them,

my wife, Helen,
my God-given soul mate and, gratefully, my personality
opposite—without whose inspiration and encouragement
this book would never have been finished,

and to the courageous couples who allowed me the privilege of
joining them in their marital dreams and struggles.

Ron Shackelford
Mission Viejo, California

CONTENTS

SERIES FOREWORD

The interface between psychology, religion, and spirituality has been of great interest to scholars for a century. In the last three decades, a broad general interest has developed in books that make practical sense out of the sophisticated research on these three subjects.

So this series, wisely urged by Praeger Publishers, intends to define the terms and explore the interface of psychology, religion, and spirituality at an operational level of daily human experience. Each volume identifies, analyzes, describes, and evaluates a range of issues, of both popular and professional interest, that deal with the psychological factors at play in the way spirituality functions within humans, and in the ways that spirituality and religion are shaped and expressed. The primary interest is psychological.

These books are written for the general reader, local library, and undergraduate university student. They are also of significant interest to the informed professional, particularly in corollary fields. The volumes in this series have great value for clinical settings and treatment models.

This series editor has spent his professional lifetime focused specifically upon research into the interface of psychology, religion, and spirituality. These matters are of the highest urgency in human affairs today, when religious motivation seems to be playing an increasing role, constructively and destructively, in the arena from personal and social ethics to national politics and world affairs.

It is just as urgent that we discover and understand better the psychological forces empowering people of genuine spirituality to give themselves to all the creative and constructive enterprises that, throughout the centuries, have made human life the humane, ordered, prosperous, and aesthetic experience it can be at its best. Surely, the forces for good in both psychology and spirituality far exceed the powers and proclivities toward the evil that we see so prominently in our world today.

This series of Praeger volumes is dedicated to the greater understanding of psychology, religion, and spirituality, and thus to the profound understanding and empowerment of those psychospiritual drivers that can help us transcend the malignancy of our pilgrimage and enormously enhance the majesty of the human spirit, indeed, the potential for magnificence in human life.

J. Harold Ellens, Ph.D.
Series Editor

Chapter 1

WHY OPPOSITES *ARE* MEANT FOR EACH OTHER

See two lovers walk down the street,
She trips, he comforts, "Careful, my sweet."
Now wed they tread the very same street,
She trips, he murmurs, "Pick up your feet!"

—Anonymous

In the beginning, "opposites attract." Yet the initial magic of attraction usually disappears over time in the daily grind of dealing with differences, which cause most marital unhappiness. In marital therapy, my observation is that the most common cause of discontent is *personality* difference, not *gender* difference. Couples frustrated with differences are *not* from opposite planets—they are typically from opposite personality zones. I suggest that couples set their focus not on solving the "riddle of sexuality," but on a more realistic, this-planet kind of quest: *to better understand my mate's strange, if not mysterious, personality approach.*

THE PROBLEM: PERSONALITY BLIND SPOTS

We all have blind spots. Just as the dark side of the Moon revolves constantly away from Earth, so our natural personality approach renders us blind to the proficiencies of other approaches. While we intend to be fair-minded, the two-sided coin of personality orientation leaves us naturally biased against proficiencies that are not our own. In marriage, these blind spots represent a shadowy flip side that can sometimes feel strangely competitive or "oppositional." How does this happen?

Personality strengths emerge from preferences that have been conditioned by use over time. Consider the analogy of your two hands. You may be a right-handed person, but you possess the same equal, boundless potential in your left hand as you do in your right. That latent potential lies dormant as long as you continue to repetitively use your right hand, further developing and honing its deft abilities. After a while, your automatic thinking leads you to fall into the belief that the right hand is "*the* best approach."

In personality functioning, our automatic belief is that our personality approach is "*the* best approach." In marriage, however, we are commonly faced with differing, if not antagonistic, personality approaches. According to one Myers-Briggs survey, this is because more than *half* of all couples differ in at least *two of the four basic personality functions*![1] Dispelling the darkness of our blind spot opens doors of opportunity, not only to gain insight, but also, as we shall see, even inspiration and emulation! Many of the beautiful proficiencies (described in each section) that bring admiration for one's mate can become enriching areas for *our own self-growth.*

Personalities are virtually destined to collide in the functional process of "managing" life together.

Yet psychology has failed to train us in understanding precisely *how* various personality types approach marital issues. This educational process can start with engaged couples reading this book *before* they get married—lest they learn in the "school of hard words"! Another place to start is training in an exciting, pioneering field destined to proliferate in the new millennium: *Emotional Quotient* or EQ. Let's take a short course in applying EQ to the marriage relationship.

Emotional Intelligence and Marital Happiness

Intelligence researchers have proven that humans possess a rich array of "intelligences" or capacities (some of which are listed in chapters 1–4). They cite, among the many kinds of intelligence, the facility or genius of *inter*personal and *intra*personal intelligence. According to researcher Daniel Goleman in his book *Emotional Intelligence,* a key measure of interpersonal intelligence is empathy. He notes, the failure to register another's feelings is a major deficit in emotional intelligence, and a tragic failing in what it means to be human. For all rapport, the root of caring, stems from emotional attunement, from the capacity for empathy. This capacity—the ability to know how another feels—comes into play in a vast array of life arenas, from sales and management to romance and parenting, to compassion and political action.[2]

The other intelligence—intrapersonal—begins around "the master aptitude of emotional intelligence," the ability to control one's emotions and delay gratification of an impulse just a little longer. Goleman cites the famous Stanford study called "the marshmallow challenge," where four-year-olds were tested for impulse control, and tracked 12 to 14 years later. Those who were able to practice self-control at age four were later found to be more self-reliant, socially competent, trustworthy, and confident than their marshmallow-grabbing friends.[3]

This ability is integral to empathy as well. Goleman notes, "Every strong emotion has at its root an impulse to action. Managing those impulses is basic to emotional intelligence.... Over-heated, over-reactive feelings only serve to impede the care for others and one's self. Yet in love relationships, managing emotions finds its highest challenge, since some of our deepest needs are at stake—to feel loved and respected or be rejected and emotionally deprived." He notes in marriage that intrapersonal intelligence takes the form of competency to

> be able to calm down (and calm your partner), empathy, and listening well.
> The most powerful form of nondefensive listening is empathy: hearing feelings behind what is being said. This requires that one partner calm down to the point where he or she is receptive to their own physiological base and try to attune or harmonize with the partner's frame of reference.[4]

Both interpersonal and intrapersonal intelligence is important to marriage because empathy is, as explained by Goleman, "the fundamental people skill." In marriage, the essential "intelligence" required is the *capacity to understand* the other's world in relation to *one's own world.* Empathy becomes the single most important skill in the evolution of a marriage because at its heart, marriage is an emotion-based understanding between two partners. By gaining a deeper understanding of the personality approach of your mate as presented in this book, your empathy level will take a giant leap forward!

But We Are So Different!

I know from personal experience that living with someone who has a befuddling or "contradictory" approach can sometimes be a grind. My wife, Helen, and I are different in *all four of the functional areas* to be discussed! But here's the good news: living with an opposite doesn't *have* to be a grind! "Irreconcilable differences" may be the legal terminology used in California to justify divorce, but that is not confirmed by marital research (psychology) or the beliefs of most religions (theology). In psychology, Gottman's research has confirmed that many marriages succeed with quite different styles of relating.[5]

The Spirituality in Every Marriage

In fact, most of the world's religions affirm that growth in spirituality comes *in the midst* of struggle. When differences create conflict, healthy couples possess a buoyant *belief* system (or faith) in their relationship, such as that found in this premise:

All problems contain within them the seed of opportunity.

Nevertheless, personality clashes can prompt me to stop *believing* in my mate and our relationship, developing instead a *contempt* for her approach. By doing this, I have crossed over both a spiritual and psychological boundary by critiquing her *person* instead of her *behavior. (Note: Throughout the book, I assume that one's mate has no pathological or severe character defects. Therefore, the differences I am talking about are solely personality based. If a character pathology or dysfunctional belief system is present, see a professional therapist or pastor, respectively.)* The spiritual terminology for this boundary jumping or trespassing is "judging." Judging is a forbidden spiritual (and psychological) position, for as one Scripture warns ominously, "For with the judgment you use, you also will be judged." The Splinter Principle further establishes the same boundary: "First take the log out of your own eye, and then you will see clearly to take the splinter out of your brother's eye."

Healthy spirituality within a marriage maintains a spirit of respect, a boundary that banishes contempt. In each chapter, you will find multiple opportunities to restore your equilibrium of respect as you "see" more clearly and profoundly your mate's inborn "intelligences." Research has established that healthy marriages major in affirming these "cherishable" qualities. Dr. John Gottman of the University of Washington found in his research that strong marriages encounter *five* positive experiences to every *single* negative experience of their mate.[6]

How to Cultivate More Positive Experiences—and Avoid Marital Therapy!

As we have seen, the "intelligence" of empathy is crucial to a deeper love relationship. This is because love is an act of the will—to constantly seek a more empathetic understanding of another. In an evolving, intimacy-developing relationship, empathetic partners make an effort to search for the sources behind their conflict. I suggest that couples will lessen conflict and enjoy more positive experiences with one another by living according to this premise:

Conflict is typically created by differing personality approaches, not because there is something wrong or deficient in my mate.

I guarantee that the quest to discover hidden strengths in your opposite's *personality* will bring new passion and spiritual energy to your relationship.

HOW DIFFERENCES BECOME OPPORTUNITIES

Think back to the days of your courtship. Remember how energized you were by the attraction of your significant other (who may be driving you crazy now!). One reason was that you felt motivated to venture outside of your own comfort zone. You opened your mind and heart to the approach of the other. During your dating days, fresh dimensions of being were uncovered like buried treasure. The world seemed larger and full of adventure. You felt great as you stepped out and tried it, crossing new thresholds! As Elizabeth Barrett Browning put it:

I love you, not only for what you are,
But for what I am when I am with you.
I love you, not only for what you have made of yourself,
But for what you are making of me.

The exciting promise of growth is present whenever you feel adventurous and step across the threshold of a new dimension of being! This promise is present every day as you interact with a mate who functions with a different personality approach! Why? Because they live out before our very eyes the proficiencies or "intelligences" that would be otherwise hidden from us. This perspective is a virtual gold mine of opportunity to any person who is committed to personal growth!

Good News: *Every* Personality Contains Hidden Proficiencies!

Modern psychology affirms that each of us is wonderfully made, possessing uncanny facility for adroitly doing something. This proficiency is imbedded in our personality at birth. I call it a "curious *felicitas*" or curious facility that is God-given. Hence, I use the term *personality preference* in this book in its broadest sense: every personality approach has an intrinsic "intelligence" or admirable proficiency *in some particular dimension of life.*

This means that your opposite possesses a curious facility for doing something that does not come naturally or easily to you. How intriguing! Residing in your mate lies a God-given genius, or at the very minimum, a curious proficiency *that you yourself do not possess.* Transformation comes when you consider these differences as opportunities for appreciation and self-development!

When an astronomer looks at the sky, a botanist views my garden, and a doctor observes his patient, they see far more than I. While my sight is limited, provision for expanding my vision is found in my mate, who is perfectly "fitted for me." *Precisely because she is my personality opposite,* she is able to enhance my appreciation of realms of human potentiality that otherwise lay beyond my awareness. She becomes my astronomer, botanist, and physician!

The "Apostle" You Live With

Driving down the road, I glance at my mirrors to see everything around me. But there is a problem: my mirror system has a blind spot. In like manner, my personality renders me unwittingly blind to the intelligence of my opposite's "strange" approaches. When I employ empathy, which breeds respect instead of contempt, Helen becomes God's mouthpiece. She is the "apostle" I live with, as illustrated by this story told by Scott Peck:

There was once an old monastery that had fallen upon hard times. Centuries earlier, it had been a thriving monastery where many monks lived and worked and had great influence on the realm. But now only five monks lived there, and they were all over seventy years old. This was clearly a dying order.

A few miles from the monastery lived an old hermit who many thought was a prophet. One day as the monks agonized over the impending demise of their order, they decided to visit the hermit to see if he might have some advice for them. Perhaps he would be able to see the future and show them what they could do to save the monastery.

The hermit welcomed the five monks to his hut. When they explained the purpose of their visit, the hermit could only commiserate with them.

"Is there anything you can tell us," the abbot inquired of the hermit, "that would help us save the monastery?"

"No, I'm sorry," said the hermit. "I don't know how your monastery can be saved. The only thing that I can tell you is that one of you is an apostle of God."

The monks were both disappointed and confused by the hermit's cryptic statement. For months after their visit, they pondered the significance of the hermit's words. As they contemplated in this manner, the monks' behavior began to change. They began to treat each other with extraordinary respect on the off chance that one of them might actually be an "apostle of God." And on the off chance that each monk himself might be "the apostle" spoken of by the hermit, each monk began to treat himself with new esteem.

Because the monastery was situated in a beautiful forest, many people came there to picnic on its tiny lawn and to walk on its paths, and even now and then to go into the tiny chapel to meditate. As they did so, without even being conscious of it, they sensed the aura of extraordinary respect that now began to surround the five old monks. It seemed to radiate out of them, permeating the atmosphere of the place. There was something strangely attractive, even compelling about it. Hardly knowing why, people began to come back to the monastery more frequently to picnic, to play, and to pray. They began to bring their friends to show them this special place. And their friends brought their friends.

As more and more visitors came, some of the younger men started to talk with the old monks. After a while one asked if he could join them. Then another. And another. Within a few years the monastery had once again become a thriving order. Thanks to the hermit's gift, it regained its former place as a vibrant center of light and spirituality throughout the realm.

("The Rabbi's Gift," as it appears in M. Scott Peck's Prologue from *The Different Drum* [New York: Simon & Schuster, 1987]; used by permission.)

Are you wise enough, like the old monks, to practice the perspective of *extraordinary respect* toward your opposite, who just might be an "apostle of God" for you?

In summary, yes, opposites do initially attract—and later repel! But do not dismay. I will show you evidence that there is a master plan afoot—to mold you into a more *whole, complete person.*

Exciting areas of potential growth lie just ahead for you!

Chapter 2

DECISION MAKING: THE FEELER VS. THINKER COLLISION

Robert and Rhonda frequently get aggravated at each other when making a parenting decision. Rhonda considers Robert an unfeeling hard-liner, who often doesn't appear to value a close, comfortable father-son relationship. On the other hand, Robert considers Rhonda a softy in discipline, who apparently doesn't value long-term parenting principles.

Robert uses a "thinker" or *reasoner* approach to decision making, while Rhonda uses a "feeler" or *relater* approach. Robert expresses *the typical reasoner's complaints about relaters* in a marriage relationship:

> "She makes decisions as if everything is a personal matter."
> "She sides with family members or friends too much."
> "She's so emotional it feels hopeless to talk about principles!"

Rhonda expresses *the typical relater's complaints about reasoners:*

> "He doesn't seem to value tact or people's feelings."
> "He makes decisions as if he is a detached, heartless person."
> "He's so intellectual it feels hopeless to talk about feelings!"

All too often, reasoners and relaters engage in the "I'm right" fight, the effort to prove that the other's approach is defective in some way. Convinced that he sees the important *principles* better than she does, Robert insists that he is right. Convinced that she senses the important *relation-*

ships better than he does, Rhonda claims that she is right. Actually, both are right, but being "right" doesn't help the tone of their marriage!

The issue here is not right or wrong, but a more respectful way of treating differences. But how can you come to *respect a decision-making approach so different* from your own?

The answer is gaining a richer, deeper understanding of your mate's approach, which is often puzzling and sometimes perceived as competitive, negative, or oppositional. Due to this lack of understanding, many partners live in separate worlds. They sadly revolve around each other like wary boxers, trying to win the case for their approach being "right"—or at least being appreciated.

So, how do you take "opposition" out of the interaction of two opposites?

BREAKING THROUGH ANGST IN DECISION MAKING

Robert and Rhonda's frustration does not come from their lack of knowledge or skill in parenting. Nor does it stem from their gender difference—though it's so easy to superficially and erroneously blame that! Their frustration comes from the lack of an empathetic appreciation of the other's approach—an appreciation you will gain as you read through this chapter.

To discern the approach you and your mate tend to use in decision making, read through the chart below. Virtually everyone will fall into one of these two categories. It shows what goes on inside the heads of reasoners and relaters at a level that is often unconscious and automatic.

Relater	*Reasoner*
(More often women, but not always)	(More often men, but not always)
Naturally values:	*Naturally values:*
people's feelings and harmonious relationships	people's principles and harmonious ideas
peace-seeking, comfort	truth-seeking, reason
friendship, sensitivity	objectivity, knowledge
Believes people are probably right without questioning their reasoning.	Questions the positions of others, believing them quite possibly wrong.

PROFICIENCIES AND INTELLIGENCES

The Classic Relater

Most women, though not all, are relaters. If you are a relater, you believe that decisions should be based primarily on relationship values, that the feelings of the individuals involved take a higher priority than concepts. Tact is favored over confrontation. You are attuned to values such as loyalty, fidelity, and compassion because you believe they are the means to helpfulness, comfort, and harmony in relationships.

Your desire for safety and security in relationships can produce a pull toward your mate that he may regard as a need for "high maintenance," as evidenced by those frequent phone calls to "just hear the sound of your voice." These types of messages reassure you that your partner is close or accessible. (You need to know that this line of unconscious or automatic thinking is completely foreign to the value system of the reasoner, who, as we shall see, is concept centered!)

Your natural bent or motivation will be to place a high value upon relationships that a reasoner will share only to a limited degree. For example, you are drawn toward movies centered in the fascinating dynamics (your view) of relationships and how life, fate, or whatever influences them. These might be labeled romance or "chick flicks" by a reasoner, who is attracted to stories with a competitive conflict involving some action drama, the proverbial "men's" movie.

It is a common occurrence for relater secretaries in the corporate world to gather and laugh in the ladies room over their reasoner bosses' hilarious efforts to hide feelings. Such pretense invites a good laugh, like the reasoner behavior of a stoic old cowboy, who walked into a blacksmith's shop and accidentally picked up a hot horseshoe just out of the furnace. Observing the cowboy quickly drop the horseshoe in obvious pain, the blacksmith asked, "Pretty hot, huh?" "Nope," the grimacing cowboy replied, "Just don't take me long to look at a horseshoe."

Like the stoic cowboy, reasoners can easily fall into a half-alive, solely "in the head" way of living. Let's take a closer look.

The Classic Reasoner

Most men, though not all, are reasoners. If you are a reasoner, you tend to focus upon the conceptual aspects of a decision, giving higher priority to *principles* than to *people*. In weighing possible choices, you are inclined to instinctively value the process of finding the relevant principles and applying them with fair-mindedness to the situation.

Your tendency to rank your sense of the concepts involved as more important than the relater's subjective judgment can get you into trouble! (You need to know that your valuing of principles as preferable to sensitivity or awareness of feelings is a line of thinking quite foreign or even "bizarre" to a relater!)

While relaters love relational or "lack-of-feeling" jokes like the cowboy story, reasoners will enjoy stories about others who appear to lack the so-called common sense of "reason" (their way of approaching decisions). While relaters will regard " dumb-blonde" jokes as not particularly funny (or appropriate, since it could hurt a *person*), reasoners will thoroughly enjoy the antics of "empty-headed" relaters. For example, consider the one about a beggar who spoke to a well-dressed blonde walking by on Rodeo Drive, saying "I haven't eaten anything for days." She looked at him and replied, "God, I wish I had your will power."

If they even laugh at different jokes, getting relaters and reasoners together sounds like a virtually impossible task at this point, doesn't it?

If They're So Different, How Did They Fall in Love?

Wow! If these two classic opposite personality approaches are so different, how did they ever fall in love in the first place? Here are some possibilities from the deeper level of motivation, as explained through personality. Circle ones that apply to you.

She Fell in Love with His	*He Fell in Love with Her*
Strength: He is knowledgeable with a keen ability to think decisively.	*Softness:* She is kind, with a keen ability to give tender personal care.
Objectivity: She admired his fair-minded and levelheaded thinking.	*Subjectivity:* He admired her warm friendliness and easy rapport with others.
Stability: He is not prone to overreactions or easily hurt feelings.	*Stability:* She is not prone to be swayed from commitment to persons important to her.

Given these differences, it is easy to understand the gradual loss of passionate attraction that was so pronounced in the "falling-in-love" stage. It is a natural progression for a relater to move from an initial positive attraction to his decisive and knowledgeable style to the more negative opinion of him being uncaring or detached! From her perspective, he has apparently distanced himself from the relational aspects of life that are so vitally important to her. And from his perspective, her wonderful warmth that once added such a spark to his life has been mysteriously transformed into irrational or impossible emotionality!

Solely because of the pull of their personalities, they are experiencing the following distress:

She Is Now Distressed by His	*He Is Now Distressed by Her*
desire to judge or detach from others	desire to protect or indulge others
apparent lack of caring or ability to show compassion readily	apparent lack of reason or inability to express logical thoughts easily
cynical attitude toward people that he "should" care about	apathetic attitude toward truth that she "should" care about

While it is initially hard for each party to accept, *both* decision-making approaches are effective, powerful, and efficient! But, you object, how can your mate's approach be just as effective as yours? Basically, it is because each has developed a high level of decision-making expertise after using this particular method for so many years! If you had used your partner's approach for the same period of time that he or she has, you would be just as effective with that approach!

So never minimize the wisdom inherent in your partner's "strange approach." After all, you may be blind to certain dimensions of a decision that your partner sees. If two heads are better than one, then it makes powerful good sense to respect—and incorporate into the joint decision—the position taken by both approaches.

When respect is present, two decision-making approaches are always wiser than one!

I persuaded Robert and Rhonda to revisit their approach to parenting their son—looking through a different lens. Using their new understanding of each other's personality strengths and weaknesses, they agreed that there was more wisdom in the approach of the other and more blindness in their own than previously seen. Robert agreed to take more of a relater role, becoming more sensitive to his son's feelings and more committed to greater closeness in their relationship. Rhonda agreed to take more of a reasoner role, becoming less influential in her son's decisions and more committed to greater valuing of his individuality.

Another interesting phenomenon took place in their relationship. With a new appreciation for the motivations and strengths of the other, they began to look less at the other's flaws and more toward areas of their own development. They discovered the power of the Splinter Principle, one of the most overlooked relationship principles in marriage. It is the simple but profound first priority in a relationship: "take the log out of your own eye *first.*" Once focus shifted to their own "logs," their level of frustration dropped dramatically. I enabled this shift toward the vast potential areas of self-development with the "Growth Possibilities" chart below. Some might call it a "motivational gift" list, based upon the natural "intelligence" or bent of each approach.

Consider the magic of taking your mate's supposed dastardly splinters and transforming them into intriguing areas of *potential growth for you*! Perhaps it could be part of a higher plan for you to develop in the following areas:

GROWTH POSSIBILITIES

Special Personality Proficiencies or "Intelligences"

Reasoners	*Relaters*
are gifted with the genius of reasoning	are gifted with the genius of relating
can tackle complicated issues or problems with incredible depth of understanding and application of knowledge (adroit reasoning ability can amaze).	can perceive the emotional messages people send with incredible depth of understanding and application of tactful diplomacy (adroit sensitivity to people can amaze).
are adept at asking questions to bring out greater clarity or truth	are adept at bridging or bringing people together for friendship or their welfare
are good at *truth* in sense of what is appropriate in an abstract, logical, or organized sense	are good at *truth* in sense of what is appropriate in an interpersonal sense of harmony, teamwork, or friendship
are proficient in critiquing a society's habits, beliefs, and methods, and finding a reasoned solution or understanding of systemic societal problems	are proficient in sensing what is right in a society/group, and joining a group or movement to serve those ends that contribute to its welfare
are often proficient as troubleshooters, rising to the needs of the occasion	are often proficient as facilitators of good working relationships, leading teams
remain calm during crises and have cool-headed, relaxing effect on others	remain tolerant, appreciative, and encouraging of cooperation and harmony

THE CHERISHING FACTOR

(Qualities that you appreciate, enjoy, and affirm as you experience and benefit from your mate. Circle those that apply.)

Reasoner

Relater

Logical, realistic—thoughtful, helpful, constructive problem solving. One receives no such focused, personalized help anywhere else in the world! (This is the harmonious teamwork she envisioned their "strong partnership" would become when they got married!)

Devoted, loyal—unswerving commitment, support, and belief in their mate. One receives no such deeply personal affirmation and emotional backing and support anywhere in our often cruel and harsh world! (This is an endearing joy and benefit of a strong partnership with a fiercely loyal mate—often a surprising joy to reasoners!)

Expedient: tries to deal with factual realities with prompt thought and action! Around-the-house problems that someone without confidence might procrastinate are resolved or quickly attended to. This can be taken as a sign of a strong desire to please or help the other and be a loving "helpmate" (of high value to a relater!).

Expressive, compassionate: you don't have to wonder what she is feeling—no secrets! Such ready expressiveness and directness can be an endearing, pleasant, enjoyable mode of communicating to a reasoner who appreciates integrity, straightforwardness, and the freshness that comes through candor (of high value to a reasoner!).

Perceptive of others' thoughts and brings pragmatic approach to helping them. Can be wonderfully loving through small acts!

Perceptive: keenly aware of mate's mood and gently and kindly concerned about it. Can magically lift your spirits when down!

Decisive, objective: tries to be fair-minded, independent, and respectful in approach to treating children and others.

Warm, energetic with family, and may express love with tireless or restless devotion to duties.

Good at "cutting through the fat" of tangential details in conversations and coming back to the central point. Enjoy the benefit of a clear, focused mind!

Good at "breaking the ice" of awkward social settings with friendly gestures and warmhearted "opening" conversation. Enjoy the benefit of an open, giving heart!

Often thoughtful and action-driven to help by conceiving solutions to root problems and banishing them.

Extraordinarily sensitive to others who are hurting, lonely, afraid, or overwhelmed.

Great problem solvers and persons of systematic analysis, often painstaking. Intensely self-determined to conceive of helpful ways and means of improving our world through wisdom, logic, and intellect. Our world needs more of them!

Great champion of the underdog, persons often cast aside. They believe in people and the possibility of change and a better future through imagination and appreciation of human potential. Our world needs more of them!

Growth Possibilities Chart for Relaters and Reasoners

She Needed to See His Strengths as Her Need to Gain Appreciation for	*He Needed to See Her Strengths as His Need to Gain Appreciation for*
Growth in capacity to gain and retain knowledge and use it decisively	Growth in capacity to feel compassion for others and use it sensitively
For example: She grasped the principles of this book and immediately applied them to her relationship with Robert.	*For example:* He opened his heart to the principles of this book and sensitively applied them to his relationship with Rhonda.
Adding reason-based thought and questioning to her process of forming conclusions about others	Adding feeling-based emotion and concern as important to his process of relating more warmly to others
For example: Improving her capacity to set and hold healthy boundaries with others rather than typically saying "yes"	*For example:* Improving his capacity to practice a healthy level of empathy for others rather than typically judging

(See the end of the chapter for some more practical suggestions.)

The "Tin Man" Syndrome

Every night in countless households across America, this scene is played out. She feels like having a conversation with him. He doesn't feel like having a conversation with her. She wants to engage his attention. He wants to be engaged doing something else. It is a classic *reasoner-relater* type of collision.

"At times it feels like I'm talking to a brick wall. I get no response from him," Rhonda complained to me. "He goes silent, and I don't know where he is. It's like trying to connect to a ghost." I call this frequent reasoner behavior the "Tin Man" Syndrome, thinking of the poor man in *The Wizard of Oz,* who lamented to Dorothy that he was "without oil." When the outer metal armor of a reasoner starts to clank for lack of expressive emotion, the relationship-sensitive relater is likely to react negatively. His retreat into silence or activity only serves to aggravate her more. As she gets more upset, he retreats further and further into his armor, trying to find protection.

Moving from his own frame of reference, the reasoner thinks (and wistfully hopes) that his retreat will "cool off the heated atmosphere." This would work for him, but unfortunately, it often does the opposite because the relater may take the lack of words personally, speculating, "What did I say or do?" Or she may grumble, ruminate, or worry about the relationship, wondering, "Why is he distancing himself from me?"

John Gray *(Men Are from Mars, Women Are from Venus,* Harper Collins Publishers, 1992) attributes this dynamic to gender, saying that men are not as self-disclosing as women. While this is generally true, there are many times when women choose to hide their feelings or thoughts from their mate as well. And sometimes the reasoner in a marriage is the woman, not the man. Moreover, blaming gender leaves us with little ground for making practical changes.

A second possible explanation is found in the research of John Gottman *(Why Marriages Succeed or Fail,* Simon and Schuster, 1994), who noted this dynamic in his discussion of "stonewalling." He calls stonewalling the act of a mate going silent, removing oneself from discussion and turning into a fortresslike stone wall. When done to communicate a defiant or angry message in an argument, it conveys disapproval, icy distance, and smugness. Gottman attributes the tendency of men to do this more often than women to cultural training (85 percent of stonewallers are men, per his research). Males emerge from childhood trained for "action," which at times means the repression of acute sensitivity to emotion.

This action orientation does, however, teach them one sensitivity: it prepares them for "adrenaline-needed" situations. Gottman theorizes that due to this conditioned physiology, researchers find that a male's blood pressure and heart rate rise much higher and stay elevated longer than their spouses. In an attempt to ward off the threat of troubling short-term explosions—with their great discomfort—men sense their vulnerability to stress-activating words of emotion.

Gottman notes that the stonewalling male is more likely of the two to be thinking or processing negative thoughts that tend to keep them riled up. "If you could read their minds, you might hear phrases like, 'I don't have to take this crap,' or 'It's all her fault.' Such inner scripts, whether of righteous indignation or innocent victimization, are clearly not self-soothing."[1]

Is there a way to change those agitating inner scripts or "automatic thinking" patterns? Clearly, it is ineffectual to put on more armor to defend against what many reasoners come to consider the "opposition." The effective way is to seek a deeper understanding of our opposite that results in more specific, practical, and positive ways of relating, as defined at the end of each chapter.

A MORE PRACTICAL APPROACH TO DIFFERENCES

Laying aside all the speculation about gender and culture-based differences, I believe it is more helpful to look at specific personality approaches to solve conflict. Focusing upon what is behind *specific personality behaviors* is a great starting place for coming up with *practical solutions that really work*!

For example, with a deeper understanding of the dynamic created in a *reasoner-relater* coupling, we can practically understand the dynamics of how the common "tin man collision" is set up—and do something about it. The reasoner mate is more comfortable in the thinking mode, and is *far* more comfortable processing *thoughts* than feelings. On the other hand, the relater is *far* more comfortable with *feelings* than thoughts. The relationship-centered relater is going to be constantly vigilant for signs of distancing in the relationship. Her bent is intimacy with her mate, and she is typically the first to notice and complain about problematic areas that threaten intimacy. She will become distressed when she receives messages that seem to convey he is moving away from her, or becoming more obscure and difficult to know—even to himself. (If the latter is the case, she is typically highly motivated to render him help.)

What can a relater do to encourage her tin man to take off his armor and share more of his inner person with her? Read carefully my tips in the following section. But for now, reasoners must come to grips with the Tin Man Paradox: *by avoiding conflict, you intensify conflict*. Once you understand the paradox, it makes sense that the most reasonable way to end the discomfort is *go toward it!* And the best way to extend the duration of the seemingly personal criticism of a relater is *to try to run away from it!*

How do you go *toward* it? Here's how to build up your marriage bank account, according to researcher Gottman:

> in stable marriages partners tend to view each other through "rose colored" glasses. They assume that each other's positive characteristics are an intrinsic part of their personality rather than occasional flukes... in unhappy marriages, partners become conditioned to look for and react to negatives in the other, and this becomes a self-fulfilling prophecy.[2]

The marital bottom line is this: The way you frame your mate is the critical engine that will exacerbate your marital mood toward the positive or the negative.

If building a positive mental "filter" toward the other is critical, how does one do it? The power of the *Married to an Opposite* approach is in its ability to continually empower your filter to color your mate as over-whelmingly *gifted and wonderful!* Your filter is so positive that negatives become inconsequential! You color your mate with "rose-colored" glasses: *yet the coloring is not contrived, but based in reality!* These gifts are wired in, deeply embedded, life-long qualities to enjoy as the years go by—because they *exist in reality.* They won't go away. They remain to be cherished and even emulated as both of you develop as persons.

To begin the cherishing process, just start with an affirmation. Take a "proficiency" off of the previous list, and offer it as an affirmation.

TEACHING THE ART AND SKILL OF AFFIRMATION

Affirmation is stating a confirmed fact. When a fact is stated positively, it is validated, and by speaking it we make it more real. Because we are aware that our mate sees us in a different way than we see ourselves, we leap ahead in self-assurance when our mate affirms us in areas where we suspect we are strong! Affirmation is the powerful, gravity-defying agent of this freeing leap. It calls forth deeper, untapped dimensions of ourselves that may not be fully realized. As an example of this positive labeling, Jesus verbally named Peter "the Rock" long before he actually became a paragon of faith. Crystallizing an opposite's potential through affirmation is every mate's job! Competition in the relationship must die, replaced by dedication to affirmation.

Anyone can follow the three simple rules of affirmation. First, it must be *genuine,* not flattery. Second, it must be *factual,* not fabricated. Third, it must be about the other's *person,* not just their role or behavior. For example, "I love the beautiful way you love Tiffany. You have the feeler gift of tenderness," is preferable to "You are a good mom. Keep up the good work."

What if the other person rejects your gesture of affirmation? With Helen, I tell myself that it is the truth, whether she initially receives it well or not. If it is a fact about her that I have observed, it is still true—even if she has a tendency to minimize it—and I will continue to period-ically mention it.

For the receiver, the art of affirmation is calmly saying "thank you" and letting the words sink in. This can be hard for reasoners, who look for ulte-rior motives, or relaters afraid of appearing pretentious. But rise above these personality tendencies and let the power of affirmation ring true inside of you, having its full, self-actualizing effect! If the affirmation is about a God-given personality proficiency, you cannot deny it or get puffed up about it anyway, since you had nothing to do with it! Because we were "wondrously made" in our mother's womb, we should never turn away from our mate's words that affirm who we really are.

Let the strength bombardment began! Make a commitment to affirmation, for in the grind of everyday differences, the tearing down is all too easy! Affirm your opposite as quickly as you can, as spontaneously as you can, as often as you can. Remember the research data for a healthy marriage: five positive experiences for each negative one is the requirement to keep the emotional accounting meter on "satisfied."

Usually it is different personalities that create conflict, not flaws in persons. When in conflict, look for a deeper understanding of personality first.

PRACTICAL PRINCIPLES FOR REASONERS AND RELATERS

Note: Always be willing to practice the *kenosis* principle: understanding empathy. In decision-making efforts, that means taking the initiative to temporarily set the comfort of your own approach aside. We do this in order to enter more profoundly into the approach of another. For example, Christians believe Christ modeled this principle when He set aside his "divine prerogatives" (*kenosis* is the Greek word in Philippians 2:6, often translated "emptied himself") and entered into our human frame of reference. This powerful act enabled Christ to love us humans more intimately and effectively.

In the same way, Buddha left the comforts of his palace privileges behind and took on a disguise as a common peasant to live with the people of his realm. In so doing, he learned things about his people that he would never have learned staying in his palace.

We can also do this, for a short time, by first making the effort to experience the world as our partner experiences it. After this has been accomplished, then move to the second step of negotiating an acceptable middle ground that acknowledges the validity and truth of both approaches.

Kenosis is the decisive pathway of the will. Once we are willing to set aside the prejudice of limited sight due to our personality bias, the pathways of mind and heart open to deeper understanding. It is the ultimate psychological and spiritual definition of *love:* the willingness to set self or "ego" aside for the sake of another.

Principles for a Reasoner Interacting with a Relater

Relational Principle 1

At its core essence, a quality marriage is almost totally open to sharing and hearing "feelings." Openness, not denial, of the importance of feelings is a characteristic of an authentic partnership in which mates are helping and enhancing each other's lives.

Personality Precept 1   *Go toward the feelings!*

Reasoners must first understand that relaters are better at gauging and managing relationships. They are well worth listening to, even if they are emotional, aggressive, or personally attacking because they may see or understand something that is affecting the relationship that you don't. While listening may be difficult for reasoners when a mate is angry, to do so is an act of love. And now comes the hardest part of all for those reasoners who tend to be tin men: *Go toward the unhappiness in order to end it!*

Do not do what Gray calls going into a "cave," and Gottman calls "stonewalling." Do not become what I call being a defensive tin man, putting on the metal armor of avoidance. Do not retract from her emotionality, no matter how irrational it may appear or be expressed.

Instead, do what your reasoner gut tells you not to do: *Go toward her feelings, even if they are angry ones!* Take her statements this way: "This issue is important to her." While it sounds like an attack on my character (remember our premise about *persons* versus *personalities*), it is really about figuring out a way to meet her needs. See if your natural focus on problem solving through altering some specific behaviors will satisfy her. If specific changes do *not* satisfy her, don't stop here: listen for deeper feelings—the root cause of her distress. While this is the hardest part for a tin man, believe that it is self-expansive and healthy for you. And, it's great for the relationship: *Go toward the anger—or whatever distressed emotions are expressed!*

For example: "I sense you are angry with me about the way I hang up my pants...but I sense that there is something else. Is there?"

"Well...yes. I feel like I'm not respected. I ask you to do something, but you continue to do it the same old way. You are so self-centered! You not only don't care about all the work I do ironing your pants, but I feel like you don't care about me as a person whom you respect." While this is painful to hear, tell yourself it is good stuff because you will learn more facts that will enable you to *reasonably solve the problem!* While she is putting it in highly emotional or personalized terms, seemingly directed at you, stay in the solution mode. Be the leader, the "solution guy," and convert the negative dialogue to some positive corrective outcomes by staying in the empathy mode: *"I want to understand. I believe we can solve this problem if I can come to a better understanding of the problem. Do I hear you saying that what would make you happy is..."*

Remember Rule 1 for drawing close to relaters: *Go toward the feelings!*

It is self-expanding for you, and fosters an authentic partnership. The quality of a marriage lives and dies on feelings. Being open and vulnerable to the heights and depths of your real feelings every day makes for a soul-mating journey in which partners have the opportunity to enhance one another's lives—or make them miserable. Relaters already know this: now, so do you, Mr. Reasoner: *Go toward the feelings!*

Relational Principle 2	A healthy relationship aims for intimacy. When it is threatened or broken, timely efforts to move toward repair and restoration are critical.
Personality Precept 2	*Find a shred of connection.*

Relaters prize keeping the communication lines open. Therefore, as a reasoner, you must find a way to convey that you understand your relater's need for connection. Moreover, assure her that you value connection as well, albeit probably not to the same degree.

When decision makers are in conflict, which bothers relaters more than reasoners, the sense of connection is threatened. One specific way to *find or refind the thread of connection* is a technique that I call "searching for value." It simply means finding something with which you can "agree in principle" if you don't agree totally. It is the search for *some* value, even if small, in what the other is saying, even if one disagrees with the major argument or approach.

The benefit is that it allows the primary intimacy connector—the line of communication—to stay intact. This opens the door for "repair gestures," as researcher Gottman calls them. Intimacy suffers when one party feels forced to concede that they are wrong. It is far better to agree to disagree, a state that can affirm "value" in the other's position. In a phrase, the simple but effort-requiring rule is: *find a shred of connection.*

For example, in the case of a mate complaining about wrinkled pants, you might say, "Well, I can see how you might feel that way, since *some-*

times I am a little careless (partial agreement and finding value) in hanging up my pants." (Psychologists sometimes call this "clouding" or "fogging." Relaters call it tact or diplomacy, usually not the strong suit of reasoners!) It is a great repair mechanism when relations are moving apart because it infuses a more positive tone on dialogue that has turned negative or heated. Remember reasoners, it is a position of strength, not weakness, to agree in principle, agree in part, or find some value in the other's approach.

Reasoners typically need further development and awareness of the powerful skills of tact and diplomacy, which are usually well practiced by relaters. Take note, reasoners, of your mate's wise valuing and sensitivity in building relationship connection. Develop a deeper appreciation of these abilities, and then emulate them yourself. It is the pathway to emotional and spiritual growth!

Relational Principle 3	Research has shown that a healthy relationship is characterized by the preponderance of words and thoughts that are positive rather than negative.
Personality Precept 3	*Express what you desire rather than criticizing.*

Because relaters crave harmonious words that fuel their feelings of closeness and relational comfort, reasoners should avoid critical comments. All too often relaters take such comments personally, even when they try not to! As a reasoner, you tend to view criticism as a necessary and beneficial way of learning from the past and solving problems. While this approach works well for you, relaters are often hurt by criticism and react to it defensively.

Instead, follow this process: Simply mention—and keep mentioning—either the need or admiration for something you desire. This will better motivate your relater, who likes to feel that she is doing something for someone and enhancing a relationship. Therefore, choose a positive desire or end result that is appealing to you, that is, one that is lovely, gracious, or pure. Then, using positive and hopeful terms, express what it is that would make you very happy.

Here's a thumbnail guide that I use. With my wife, I try to make all requests with a straightforward, honest "I" statement, such as "I'd like." This forces me to take responsibility for the request by starting my proposal with the personal pronoun "I." It makes me sound less blaming, which scores zero points with relaters! Doing so will make your relater better able to hear you.

For example, I taught Robert to use "I" statements rather than his former "you" statements that seemed to place blame on Rhonda for his own unhappiness: "*You* get so involved with your ladies group that it's impossible to get away in the summer." He got much better results when he learned to express his own feelings responsibly by saying, "*I* love the High Sierra. *I* would really like to take one or two trips to the mountains this summer."

It wasn't too long before Rhonda commented that Robert seemed somewhat changed, as if he had grown less critical and easier to get along with. It seemed like a small thing to Robert, but not after he heard her say that she was delighted! "Of course," Robert said to me, "it makes sense now: she's a relater and she is more focused on the mood or tone of the relationship than I."

"I" messages allow a reasoner to breathe by saying what he desires, without trying to "walk on eggshells," worrying about a painfully emotional or personalized response. It allows him to follow Principle 3: *Express what you desire rather than criticizing.*

Relational Principle 4	A healthy soul is characterized by a willingness to give, compromise, and negotiate when needs are in conflict.
Personality Precept 4	*Find a point of agreement quickly: The longer you argue your case, the more intimacy you lose!*

Find a point of agreement as quickly as possible when dealing with a relater because they prize harmony and despise disagreement. The longer any acrimony exists, the greater the distance between you will grow. As a foolish relater, I have argued, debated, and dogmatically insisted that I was "right," even when my partner had ceased to debate! I have learned that if she begins to withdraw from the issue, she is also starting to withdraw from me!

Relaters are drained by feelings of animosity or aggression between individuals. For her, passion flourishes in clean rooms that are free of the germs of disagreement! The polarization that comes with conflict drains her of any desire to be close to her mate.

So calm your tendency to win or to use excessively strong words that will only be perceived as unhelpful combativeness by a harmony-seeking relater.

How, then, do you present your point of view? Simply state your case. Then, change your focus by making a greater effort to more deeply understand and fully appreciate your partner's side without judging her or the perspective shared. The best way to do this is by asking lots of clarifying questions like: *"Do I hear you saying ... ?"* or *"Are you saying that ... ?"*

In summary, set forth your concepts, but *do not build excessively long cases* to support your view. With relaters, *case building is distance building!* If you come away feeling that you have won and your partner has lost, guess what? Both of you have lost! Remember Principle 4: *Find a point of agreement quickly!*

Relational Principle 5	A healthy soul resists any condescending or judging attitude. Such attitudes are cancerous, not only to relational closeness, but to one's own spirit as well.
Personality Precept 5	*Don't label her an "irrational" person.*

Many married men across our land are in pain today. As a therapist, I am often saddened as I come into touch with this deep strain of hopelessness, bewilderment, and angst. These men have convinced themselves that they live with an "irrational" woman with whom they can no longer *reason.* They no longer believe that the two of them can make logical decisions or reach logical conclusions. (If you know a reasoner like this, please give him this book before he gives up completely!)

As a reasoner, you must come to understand that your relater will have a natural tendency *not to challenge other people's beliefs.* She will tend to *assume* that authorities are correct until proven otherwise. Her tendency to *avoid a great deal of critical thinking* can make her vulnerable to a reasoner's unmerited assessment that she is intellectually shallow, simple-minded, or irrational. You must avoid at all costs the temptation to label her "foolish" (e.g., see the strong words of Christ about such negative labels in the Sermon on the Mount). Never say she is "impossibly emotional." Such a "smarter-than-thou" attitude will greatly harm the relationship, putting you in a passion-killing, "parent-to-child" position.

It is better to regard the relater's lack of intense focus upon critical thinking as something that frees her to nurture her capacity for feeling close to others—a capacity that few reasoners can exercise as well as relaters! A relater is particularly able to enjoy feelings—not only comfortable feelings—with others, but a profound level of comfort within herself.

Appreciate her capacity to offer comfort, and don't discount her intellect.

On the other hand, my experience with reasoners is that a lot of them are "unsettled" with or unable to enjoy a profound feeling of "comfort." When hard pressed in therapy, often reasoners will admit that they frequently feel starved in the ability to experience the profound sense of comfort and pleasure that they admire in their relater mate. Once they come to marvel at their relater's skill in bringing the richness of pure joy and childlike play to the world, they are on the road to discovering it themselves!

As a reasoner, I know how the passionless grind of constant cognitive-based decision making can foul the engine of one's experience of life. I know many men who would love to feel more of the pure, simple pleasure of the "comfort dimension" that is so available to relaters. Only the most stubborn of reasoners would not prize the gift that his relater can bestow upon him: the capacity for more delightful, wondrous comfort!

So, rather than labeling her hopelessly "irrational" or "emotional" and discounting her intellect, sit back and marvel at her God-given capacity to feel joy, comfort, and pleasure. Wouldn't you like to experience more of these feelings? Do you want to feel more of them? Then don't label her an "irrational" person, but instead work at incorporating more of this relater proficiency into your life!

Relational Principle 6	A healthy soul mate perseveres in expressing affirmation of good qualities in another. Continue saying "I love you" or "I love your..." Do so even on days when your mind must conquer your mood.
Personality Precept 6	*Persevere with words of assurance and praise.*

As a reasoner, you may ask, "Is there any scientific data to prove that such 'sweet talk' has any real effect on a relationship?" Indeed, the PAIR Project study, conducted at the University of Texas, found in its marriage research on 168 couples that the husbands' "affectional expression" reduced the impact of early negativity on declines in their wives' satisfaction.[3]

Why is "affectional expression" so important to relater types? I suggest it is because the relater possesses such a fine-tuned inner "compass for comfort" that she needs replenishment to nourish this capacity. That replenishment comes with your affirmation of her inner and outer beauty, and your validation of her character and gifts. She needs the emotional protection, hope, and perseverance of your loving affirmation in order to feel cherished.

Therefore, the reasoner must work at being a frequent source of positive encouragement and genuine appreciation. (In this book, you'll find many new reasons to appreciate your opposite spouse.) Repeat again and again words that acknowledge her uniqueness. Be a steady source of encouragement for her. To you it may feel obvious, repetitious, and unnecessary, but to her, your words are stimulating and essential! Your appreciation of your mate replenishes her batteries and sparks the delicious pleasure of comfortable, cherished closeness with her partner.

Resist the conclusion that your mate lacks self-esteem because she needs compliments.

She is *not* codependent simply because she likes and is deeply moved by your affirming words. They move her because she is a relater. (Note: Affirmation is different from flattery. She will be highly sensitized to contrived statements because she is finely "tuned-in" to the frequency of sincere praise.) Make sure you can stand by your words of praise. If you truly believe them and feel them, you can stand her scrutiny.

Again, affirm the positive when it is true, and make such affirmation a habit!

Remember that the sincerity of the expression (heartfelt, serious) is more important than the exact words, as rough-hewn as they seem to you. Because she lives, moves, and breathes in a world energized by relationship, she *needs* your words—but exactly what kind of words?

Speak of her character and any traits that are personally endearing. Words like "sweetheart" may be passion producers. They can prompt the free expression of her inner feelings, which can often result in, among other things, great sex! Your relater needs the oxygen of your romantic words, your gifts of flowers, and your sincere affirmations.

Don't ever view these needs as weakness! Instead, follow Principle 6: *Persevere with words of assurance and praise.*

Postscript

Reasoners often overlook the intelligence found within the more emotional approach of relaters. Yet, there is intelligence *in* the emotions and the sense in which intelligence can be brought *to* the emotions.[4] The relater models many appealing proficiencies that are ripe to be picked by a reasoner who is wise enough to be intrigued by them! Go back and review the list of "intelligences," and see your mate through his/her personality gifts and motivations. Circle all the qualities that you can see manifest in the personality approach of your mate. Tell your partner that you are reading about him/her, and that it is making you more appreciative—and loving!

What Happened When Robert Applied These Rules?

When Robert started expressing his desires without criticism, Rhonda enjoyed the feel of a new calm in their relationship. He still presented his "case" in how to parent their son, but was much more open to hearing and considering her point of view. After he observed her pleased spirit whenever he voiced genuine admiration, he became more motivated to compliment her. (It felt like "cherishing" to her, and she loved it!) After seeing the positive *reasons* (and relationship fruits!) for doing so, he remained committed to doing it—whether he got an overt response, a questioning look, or whatever! He knew he was simply affirming the God-given truth about her—that was now crystallized as never before. And he was a man committed to truth!

Can small things make a big difference in a relationship?

Ask Rhonda. She told me with a big smile, "It's wonderful!"

For a Relater Dealing with a Reasoner

Relational Principle 1	A healthy (reasoner) soul invites personal growth. Honest, critical feedback from a loved one is an essential ingredient to personal growth.
Personality Precept 1	*Understand that critical feedback is given to improve, not to harm.*

You know those strong, harsh words he occasionally chooses to use? While you might never use such harsh terminology, the reasoner is often emphasizing, coloring, or dramatizing his viewpoint. This is the reasoner's way of communicating his perspective about a decision, that is, his reasoning. You must remember that a reasoner may naturally discount the relational impact of his words because relationship is not his primary focus. He is probably so focused on his principle that he has not even considered the manner of his communication. *He's probably not as insensitive as his language may suggest!*

Make a special effort not to react personally to his words.

Instead of reacting immediately to critical feedback, promise him that you will think about the point he is making. Then do so, when your feelings have calmed down and you are genuinely open to hearing the criticism. If it is offered in love and gives you a perspective you have previously been blind to, it is a gift you can be grateful for.

Aren't differences great? They certainly can be when it comes to personal growth through the benefits of two partners who become one another's most observant, loving, and intimate "coach." The Grand Designer had higher vision than ours when He merged two half-blinded souls in holy matrimony!

Relational/Spiritual Principle 2	A healthy relationship and spirituality is characterized by courageous decisiveness, not fearful timidity. Indecision is a knife that leaves a ragged edge. Decision leaves a clean cut, whether right or wrong.
Personality Precept 2	*Value his sound mind and decisive actions.*

A reasoner's sense of self comes, in large part, from his belief in his ability to think and act. He likes the feeling of confidence that comes from his mastery of reasoning and therefore feeling "on top" of the concepts being considered.

A relater, however, can easily interpret the reasoner's need to feel "on top" of the thinking process as his need to be in control. "He's a controller type," I often hear a woman complain in therapy, as if he were born that way. "He always wants to have the last word in a decision." Sometimes a man may be an aggressive, strong-willed controller, which is a character issue. But before you leap to that conclusion, consider that he might simply be a strong reasoner, who places a premium on having his ideas heard and valued. Remember our attitudinal goal when there is a decision-making clash: look for personality motivation first, character motivation second.

Reasoners want their thinking to be validated in the same way that relaters desire their feelings to be validated!

For example, whenever I get involved in a plumbing project at our house, my self-concept can rocket downward from supreme confidence to utter despair in 30 minutes or less! Why? Because my sense that I possess a sound mind and competent know-how is thrown into question. It had once appeared to be such a simple and easy task! Even the most simple-minded man should be able to do it! At this point of my plumbing project, anything that even approaches a criticism will be taken as a threat to my vulnerable ego.

When a reasoner feels incompetent, he tends to withdraw into his head. In the secure fortress of his quiet, secret, inner world, he can work at coming up with a "reasonable" perspective. He can gather all of his reasoning abilities to do battle with the demon of self-questioning. Am I competent or am I not? Am I a man or am I not? Wise relaters know that a reasoner will come out from behind his buttressed walls sooner when she understands what his is doing. Also helpful are sincere words of appreciation, particularly about his skills or jobs well done. Remind him of an appreciated decisive decision that he made, or action that he took, with its concurrent (fueling) sense of mastery.

> *It is critical to frequently give him words of admiration for his ability to "get the job done."*

Remember researcher Gottman's finding that happy marriages have five positive experiences for every negative. Why not err on the overactive side in positive verbal appreciation? For example, tell him what a great "romancer" he is when he does something you like or makes a kind gesture. Appreciate that your reasoner is particularly skilled or insightful at what he did. Fuel his sense of competence by *valuing his sound mind and decisiveness.*

You will have a more passionate man on your hands!

Relational Principle 3	A healthy (reasoner) soul possesses a dedication to truthful, factual communication. Assertive speech frees the spirit, while passive speech depletes it.
Personality Precept 3	*Speak in reasonable, specific, cause-and-effect terms when making decisions.*

Since reasoners prefer to think of reasons why something should or shouldn't be (and the more reasons the better!), start decision-making discussions with a specifically stated reason(s) for your point of view. State *why* you feel your perspective is important. For example, in dealing with their son, Rhonda would say, "I don't think that's the right approach." But she needed to go further and specifically say *why* she thought it was the wrong approach and her fears about its consequences. Being a reasoner who thinks in cause-and-effect terms, Robert was waiting for an "if...then" sequence of thoughts or feelings. If he didn't get it, he was forced to make his own translation.

Be as clear, direct, and concept-focused as you can. Use language that is specific to the issue at hand. Don't say, "Mark is worrying me. He's acting strange." Your reasoner will be waiting for some specific actions that have prompted your concerns, for instance: "Mark has been closing the door to his room a lot lately. I wonder what he is doing in there. Do you think this is a problem?"

Stick with one concept and don't bring up others until you are finished discussing the first. Dealing with too many concepts at once is irksome and unhelpful for reasoners. Such "noise"—fuzzy or unreasonable lines of thinking—will make it easier for him to tune you out!

Relational Principle 4	Healthy couples don't play games that "test" the other's empathy or affection.
Personality Precept 4	*Give up hinting and expecting him to pick up subtle, emotion-based cues. (Hinting will only frustrate both of you!)*

The reasoner is simply not as attuned to emotional cues as you are. If you express disappointment that he doesn't pick up on these cues, it will only make him more defensive or more critical of you. (Measuring his level of caring for you by playing the "hint game" is like gambling in Vegas: odds are that you will be the loser!)

Therefore, if you want to make a request, don't hint, but say it directly. For him, that means stating the *specific reasons* why you think it is a good idea, or why it would make you happy. For example, don't say, "The May Company is having a sale on sofa chairs on Saturday." Without finishing the statement with your specific request, your words will be too vague and frustrating for reasoners, who now must go through the guesswork of pondering, "Is she asking if I'm interested in buying a sofa chair or interested in going with her?" It is better to say more directly, "I want to see the sofa chairs at the May Company sale. Are you interested in coming with me?"

When making a request to a reasoner, avoid emotion-charged language (e.g., sarcasm, innuendo, negative past experiences, and so on). Stay in the "cool mode" of wishes expressed in *action-oriented terms,* without relational or emotional overtones. He will grow to love you for your calm stability—and bend over backwards to comply!

Conclusion

Trust your relater instincts! Research has proven that relaters are better than reasoners in empathy and in discerning the factors that make for a satisfying relationship. For example, one study found that a wife's premarital ambivalence predicts declines in both the wife's love and her husband's satisfaction in later years.[5] Such ambivalence should be noted carefully!

(One way to address this and find greater clarity is for couples who are seriously considering marriage to visit a Web site—like http://www.marriedtoanopposite.com—to get an in-depth printout of their respective personality approaches, motivations, and potential relational issues.) In any case, relaters typically have a more finely tuned inner sensitivity to relational factors, and should be empowered to use them.

CALM DECISION MAKING: A MASTER EMOTIONAL INTELLIGENCE

As EQ expert Goleman points out, a good mood enhances the ability to think flexibly and deal with greater complexity.[6] This makes it easier to find solutions. Happy people have a perceptual bias, partly because memory is state-specific. In a pleasant frame of mind, we remember more positive events. As we think over the pros and cons of a course of action while feeling agreeable, memory biases our weighing of evidence in a positive direction. This makes us more likely to do something slightly more adventurous or try on a different perspective or approach. When emotions get out of control, they impede intellect. Bringing mood states back into line, or what Goleman calls "emotional competence," is the master aptitude that facilitates all other kinds of intelligence.[7]

By seeking to gain a deeper understanding of our opposite, we foster this master aptitude of calming and managing our emotions as we relate to our partner. We are less prone to moodiness and negative judgment as we employ an empathetic perspective, trying to see things from another personality's point of view. For example, Robert was pleased that Rhonda seemed less reactive when he spoke about something that she would have previously considered a personal attack. Now she saw it as critical feedback given with good intentions to improve, not harm her.

As they discussed issues more calmly, the process was much more pleasant, though their differences did not go away. For Robert, it was easier because he didn't have to guess at so many things and work so hard anymore. He could hear precisely what the real issues were with Rhonda, as she tried to be more specific and use lots of reasons. She was pleased to see him make more of an effort to understand and value where she was coming from. He realized that he needed to be more aware of—and sensitive to—the feelings of his son. This made it easier for him to empathize with her perspective—rather than make a case against it—which made the decision-making process less tense for both.

Acceptance of each person's approach cleans the windshield for better insight past the dirt and distortion of our particular biases. We are vulnerable to certain common errors, such as the following characteristics of relaters and reasoners.

CLASSIC ERRORS OF EACH TYPE

The Personalization Error

Relaters are often tempted to take—usually with a self-depreciating slant—an impersonal statement made by the reasoner as personally applicable to them. Because relaters would never state their opinion in such a harsh and grating way unless they really meant it, they tend to take his words to heart. If you are a relater, you question yourself, wondering how *you* have somehow failed. Vulnerable to words by virtue of your keen sensitivity to people, you can easily feel unloved, unappreciated, or devalued.

This automatic personalization is an error in thinking that relaters may not even be conscious of. Simply put, you see yourself as the cause of some negative event that, in fact, you did not cause. This so-called "cognitive distortion" is based on a hidden bias in your automatic pattern of thinking. It is revealed in the following progression ("global-thinking" pattern) in a relater's potential self-talk:

"I wonder why he doesn't care about my opinion."

"I feel like my needs are always devalued."

"I don't feel cherished anymore."

"I need someone who really cares for me."

"I want a divorce!" (The personalization error can be devastating to your passion!)

The antidote to the personalization error is called "checking the evidence." It requires the courage to challenge or verify your automatic thought patterns. I taught Rhonda to slow down her natural reactivity to Robert's statements by using paraphrasing or clarifying statements such as: *"I hear you saying that..."* or *"Are you saying that...?"*

Example

Rhonda: (Paraphrasing) "Are you saying that—you don't like the way I make salad?"

Robert: "No, they're okay. I just don't like eating salads every single night."

After paraphrasing, she added in the "possible" negative interpretation that she thought she heard in the statement. Like Rhonda, check the evidence: find out if your negative interpretation is correct—or cognitively distorted.

When Rhonda started challenging her automatic thinking by asking clarifying statements, she found out something that delighted her. Most of the time, Robert was not intending to convey anything personally directed at her! And on the rare occasions when he was, she was now able to deal with it because she could understand the specific behavior that troubled him. She could focus on changing the behavior—rather than trying to change him. That made them both feel a lot better!

Moreover, in Robert's automatic thinking pattern, it hadn't occurred to him that matters in this category could be taken so personally by a very sensitive relater.

The Impersonalization Error

On the mirror side is the occasionally distorted thinking of the reasoner. His tendency is to occasionally err on the side of insensitivity to the possible personalized interpretation of his statements. The impersonalization error means being unaware of the potential pain inherent in your messages—particularly to relater types.

As a case in point, using his typical concept-centered approach, Robert had unconsciously ignored the potential emotional impact of his words and tone of voice—he considered them as peripheral to his point. When occasionally Rhonda would blow up over his "lack of sensitivity," he would become frustrated, telling me, "I've got to walk on eggshells around her because she takes things so personally. She's so emotional."

Rather than having Robert continue to walk on eggshells, I taught him how to assertively state his opinion or ask for some things without hurting feelings by making clear "I" statements rather than indirect, passive statements. By implementing assertive (not aggressive) statements that start with the pronoun "I" instead of making aggressive "you" statements, he learned to state opinions without betraying his commitment to integrity and truthfulness. He not only pleasantly surprised Rhonda with his newfound sensitivity, but also he discovered at work that fellow employees moving up in the organization paid keen attention to this awareness and skill. While the old Robert might have resisted such "sensitivity training," he decided to take the higher road—learn a new skill—and expand himself.

RELATERS, REASONERS, AND "PSEUDOSUBMISSION"

Marriages fall into various styles of relating, and many of them are quite successful. One common style is the traditional, hierarchical, structured style of male "headship." Most religions foster the male headship role, and many Christians consider this the only biblical model (not true). The implication is that marital satisfaction is directly correlated to the quality of the wife's submission to her husband, the "head."

In the case of Robert and Rhonda, both parties were tempted to fall into a distorted use of this "headship" model. While it is common for marital therapists to hear dysfunctional couples justify their approach as following this model, there is a subtle and vitally important difference between "pseudosubmission" and the real McCoy.

The pseudosubmission version is used as a rationalization whenever communication deteriorates into the passive mode, in which both parties allow their deeper needs to go unexpressed. They choose to interact at a superficial level. As time passes, they become strangers, living in separate emotional worlds because intimacy can only flourish in the oxygen of authenticity.

While pseudosubmission may *feel* like loving submission, it is a fantasy. The mark of real submission is a genuine expression of needs, where genuine differences and conflicting wishes are verbalized clearly and well known to both parties. How is each personality type tempted to fall into a passive or superficial level of communication because of their approach?

The reasoner is prone to view headship as pertaining to decision making, as in "the buck stops here," and "somebody has to be in control." Therefore, he is quick to conceptualize this model as *made for a person of his talents!* After all, of the two persons, he is the one who is best at being objective, decisive, and tough-minded with the principles and concepts involved in decision making.

On the other hand, the relater can be prone to view headship as pertaining to submission, as in "spirituality is about sacrifice," and "someone has got to be submissive." Therefore, she is quick to feel like this model was *made for a person of her talents!* After all, of the two mates, she is the one who is best at being kind, forgiving, and tenderhearted. She is good at drawing the wide circle of acceptance of small differences that threaten the harmony "necessary" in a relationship.

The problem that therapists see evolving from the above approach, when followed over the years, is one of emotional distancing. Instead of the occasional healthy conflict where each side airs his or her repressed thoughts and feelings about a decision, the decision-making process becomes muted, shortcut, and superficial.

Because he holds a vivid distaste for unsolved problems and a disharmony of ideas, the reasoner can choose to go *passive* in communicating his genuine emotional needs. In the process, he unwittingly sacrifices his "person" for the sake of his "role" (being a "responsible head" of his family)—which to him is being the ever-strong decision maker. He shortchanges himself and the relationship.

Because she holds a vivid distaste for disharmony, the relater can choose to go *passive* in her communication as well. She starts to repress genuine feelings or thoughts that she knows will rock the boat. In the process, she sacrifices her personhood for her role as well. Like a plant suffocating under a glass jar, her inner person continues to die a slow death over time, lacking the fresh oxygen of free expression. Choosing repression is a living suicide for her—and the marriage relationship.

Real submission that honors the trust of a committed relationship, even in the midst of conflict, requires *assertive communication.* I show relaters the difference between the *passive* and *assertive* communication modes, as listed below:

Passive	*Assertive*
avoids conflict	acknowledges conflict
minimizes true feelings	stays current with true feelings
defers responsibility or risks	takes responsibility and risks

The real McCoy of true submission only happens in relationships dedicated to the truth of assertive communication. Submission has very little to do with "roles," and everything to do with being honest about differences! True spirituality in marriage will maintain the integrity of dealing with—not avoiding—authentic differences.

This raises the question: Can personality differences be used to better understand spirituality preferences? I believe they can, if used as a very rough, general guide to see oneself and possible areas for potential spiritual development. Let's take a closer look at the possible "spiritual profiles" of reasoners and relaters.

PERSONALITY TYPES AND SPIRITUAL GROWTH

Authentic spirituality is characterized by a balanced and yet robust functioning in *both* the emotional and intellectual dimensions. Any form that falls short in either dimension becomes distorted spirituality, as found in eccentric practices and extreme sects. The demanding spirituality of empathy requires a commitment to full exploration and use of our cognitive and affective facilities.

What does this mean for reasoners and relaters? Certainly, a possible starting area for charting the future growth of your spirit would be a clear acknowledgment of your proficiencies and concurrent deficiencies. While personality type does not correlate with spiritual type on a direct one-to-one basis, this section can allow you to more clearly see your innate tendencies, along with the concurrent bias of each tendency. To help set or affirm your goals for spiritual growth, circle those that apply to you:

The Relater	*The Reasoner*
Attracted to God as presented in relational context, such as family values or social interaction.	Attracted to God as presented in conceptual context, such as theological questions or search for intellectual truth.
Prefer God as a relationship-seeking figure. For example, the Father, "daddy,"—the lovable, approachable patriarch who heals brokenness of any kind, such as resolving angry/broken relationships and healing sickness.	Pulled toward God as an answer-giving entity. For example, the Creator (First Cause) or Absolute Sovereign who establishes principles, such as creating a reasonable, cause/effect universe.

The Spiritual Profile of a Relater

The relater is likely to be attracted to a spirituality that values feelings, devotion, and fidelity. If you are a relater, you particularly prize the harmony, communion, and appreciation of God found in fellowship. You value teaching that is oriented toward relationships, and find yourself moved by a spiritual message about harmony, value of family, or intimate communion with God.

Your *curiosa felicitas* or special proficiency in spirituality is ready trust, deep devotion, and a compassionate responsiveness to humans in pain. You seek the kind of idyllic spirituality found in harmony among persons who are drawn together into a seamless, unified body of one mind and heart.

Your areas for spiritual growth, which might be called your "cross," are aspects of the faith journey that don't come easily or that you'd prefer to avoid. You may, for instance, tend toward blind trust or the idealization of authority. Sometimes, you would be better off questioning authority or acting in contrary ways when asked to do something irrational (e.g., give over a large amount of money) or meet unrealistic expectations (e.g., live a perfectly pure and loving spiritual life).

Also, beware of emotional thinking, the cognitive distortion of feeling something so strongly that it *must* be unquestionably right. This can be manifest in becoming overly protective or sentimental about certain aspects of spiritual preference, such as family values overshadowing the full development of an individual's God-given gifts or personal autonomy. Emotional thinking makes it too easy to block out any contrary facts. For example, if a certain spiritual leader or movement touches your heart, you may find yourself vulnerable to a naïve, emotion-based commitment that you come to regret later.

As a relater, you may tend to rest in superficial knowledge or be content despite a lack of spiritual education. For example, you may avoid the study of Scripture or a better understanding of various religious doctrines, or asking difficult questions about issues that disturb or confuse you. You may need to aggressively confront certain spiritual concepts that you previously ignored because you felt uncomfortable with the controversy or turmoil these issues created. You may have to confront your avoidance that is rooted in your anticipated emotional anguish or the mental effort required to revise your view of God.

In summary, to experience a more robust spiritual wholeness, you may need to work on using your facility for reason to acquire more spiritual knowledge and sophistication.

The Spiritual Profile of a Reasoner

For the reasoner, spiritual reality is rooted in reason, principle, and objective values. If you are a reasoner, you are attracted to logical, cause/effect patterns of thought, and you are comfortable speculating about and analyzing abstract theological questions. You enjoy seeking truth in a cognitive, enlightened fashion, and find little satisfaction in a church tea, for example, that offers no intellectual activity. You regard a "great sermon" as one that satisfies your intellectual longing for reason and conceptual order.

The "cross" that the reasoner will tend to avoid is comprised of heartfelt devotion and/or personal compassion. You may occasionally grow apathetic, critical, or cynical, and need to develop a warmer relationship with God and His people. Work on becoming more consistent in prayer and in meeting regularly with friends or a spiritual mentor. Doing so will help you come to appreciate the spiritual blessings and interpersonal comfort that you tend to resist or question. Get involved with an issue-related class or relationship-oriented Bible study, or agree to meet regularly with a spiritual partner or friend to hold you accountable for carrying your "cross."

In general, to experience a more robust spirituality, you must develop your capacity for loyalty, devotion, and trust.

SUMMARY OF REASONERS AND RELATERS

In our laziness, it is easy to blame problems on gender. That easy "solution" can deter us from the more productive, if difficult, effort to understand a different approach. Of course, any relationship can be frustrating at times. I am reminded of a dialogue between Winston Churchill and a lady of Parliament who was his political antagonist. One day, the lady's frustration got the best of her, and she blurted out, "If I were your wife, I'd spike your tea with arsenic!" In words appropriate to the exchange of mutual frustration, Churchill retorted, "My dear lady, if I were your husband, I'd drink it!"

When it comes to decision making in marriage, being calm is crucially important. Calm comes from seeking a deeper level of understanding. This understanding enabled Robert and Rhonda to enjoy greater comfort as they dealt with the difficult task of parenting, as well as other decisions.

After reading this chapter, I suggest that couples talk about their understanding of the other's approach. The next time the frustration rises due to the thinker-feeler collision, you now have some new tools and insights that will enable you to stay calmer—and happier!

Chapter 3

LIFESTYLE APPROACHES: THE ODD COUPLE—ONE BY PLAN, ONE BY IMPULSE

Pete lays out his clothes the night before he goes fishing.
Jean picks out her clothes after her morning shower.
Pete's desk is as neat as a pin.
Jean's desk depicts "cyclone devastation."

Pete likes to plan ahead, and Jean likes to play it by ear. Pete is the "planner" type, who grumbles the usual complaints about the lifestyle approach of his "journeyer" wife:

"Why can't she plan just a little bit in advance?" Pete asks. "Everything is done at the last minute. Or, when the impulse moves her. It would drive me crazy to live like that."

Jean counters with similar complaints about Pete's approach to life:

"I would feel so hemmed in if I had to plan as much as Pete does," Jean says. "Who needs it? Life is fun when you live it now, not in some future that may not even happen. All his planning does is tie him up like a horse with side eye blinders on."

LIFESTYLE: DIFFERING WAYS TO THE "GOOD LIFE"

This "odd coupling" reflects two categorically different ways to embrace life. While there are many ways of approaching life, in general, all of us fall into one of these categories. We believe either that life is an opportunity to be *productive* or a process to be *experienced.*

For planners, a good life tries to achieve something. It should be tackled with a strong will, or otherwise precious time and energy can be wasted. If you are a planner, you prefer to willfully order and anticipate your life as an organizational task, requiring preparation, discipline, and goal setting. Like Pete, you expect that life should generally fit into your categories and unfold as you expect it to.

For journeyers, life should be experienced with an open spirit. If you are a journeyer, you prefer to let the day unfold and go with the flow. Like Jean, you prefer a life lived with flexibility and spontaneity. Each day is to be embraced with a fresh spirit because you expect every day to be different.

To get a clear picture of each life approach, I have laid out the polarities defined in the dialectic below. While the descriptions may not fit us exactly, all of us will generally fall into one of these two categories. Pick the one that best fits you.

A Planner's Life Approach	*A Journeyer's Life Approach*
goal-oriented	process-oriented
highest goal: achieving and enjoying the meaning of life	highest process: appreciating and enjoying the very experience of life
organization is important	adaptability is important
motivated not to waste time in order to be productive each and every day	motivated not to miss opportunities that may happen

"Proficiencies" and Intelligences

Planner	Journeyer
adept organizers of people or processes that are unexpected or accidental	adept at adjusting to situations
self-disciplined in achievement	flexible in dealing with change
exacting in thought process, demand clarity and lack of ambiguity	tolerant of others and situations; like the freedom to experience and try new pleasures
quick, orderly thought process; often decisive and definite opinions	quick to take in new situations and masterfully handle without undue stress

good at monitoring a task and staying with it, following through to bring things in conformity with original plan

good at monitoring new and changing information, keeping options open, and using curiosity and patience to stay open if decision may have to be changed

masters at making plans and having matters settled rather than leaving them "up in the air"

masters at changing plans and flowing with matters that are unsettled, living with the idea of waiting for more data

take great pleasure in finishing or accomplishing a goal

take great pleasure in starting a new project, until newness wears off

Cherishing Factors

Planner

Journeyer

decisive person who can take command and make good things happen: strong to be around

tolerant person who can go with the flow and make things better when they are not going well: comfortable to be with

skilled maker of long-range plans and advocate of beautiful goals: trustworthy to be with

skilled user of impulse and spontaneous motivation, advocate of improvisation: enlivening to be with

crisp, rational thinker, shares opinions: can be stimulating to listen to

light and likable, easygoing and nice: most people enjoy and can have fun with

COMMON CLASHES: VACATION, THE GYM, AND TASTING LIFE

When on vacation, Pete is "destination-oriented," meaning he wants to get there without any delays, stops, or side excursions. After all, he has been looking forward for a long time to getting out of town, savoring the picture of himself arriving at his long-awaited vacation spot. On the other hand, Jean wants to enjoy the journey, staying open to any of the pleasures or delights that happen to arise along the way. After all, she has been looking forward to a nonscheduled time, savoring the idea of free time and space.

When they head for a gym workout, Pete sticks to his standard, routine exercise process, believing in the value of staying "on task." His serious dedication to his workout goals is characteristic of the planner lifestyle approach. When Jean goes to the gym (she goes in fits and starts), she gets bored with the same process each time. Without realizing it, she is motivationally pulled by her personality to more pleasant workout experiences as advertised in the latest fitness approach or the newest equipment. In summary, if it's not a pleasant experience for Jean, then it makes great sense to her to move on to something else.

Pete believes a lifestyle based on long-term goals will yield the greatest rewards. He quotes the famous preacher Fosdick, who noted that the ancient Roman emperor Nero was fond of laughing at the long-term hopes of the Apostle Paul. But today, after centuries of time has passed, many fathers name their sons "Paul," and their dogs "Nero"!

Jean's quest is living in the "now," and she likes the adage that a camera click can ruin the pleasant *experience of the moment.* After a rainstorm had passed one day, she walked outside to a beautiful rainbow. As she watched the sun wash her backyard garden in brilliance, the colors spilled over into her senses, as if she were actually standing *in* the rainbow, transfixed in time. In her joy, she called to Pete and her daughter, who came, saw the rainbow, and returned to whatever they had been doing. Such indifference almost seemed a sacrilege, she thought, until she realized that they had seen a rainbow—but she had stood *in the rainbow.*

"Life doesn't last long," says Jean. "I want to experience every moment."

THE METAPHOR OF MONEY AS A PERSONALITY ISSUE

In relationships, there is frequently a clash over the issue of money, which is often a great metaphor for lifestyle approach values. Pete was the cautious spendthrift who preferred to plan and save with discipline. Believing there is "no gain without pain," he is the more long-term, conservative investor, preferring bonds and fixed-income types of investments to a portfolio with lots of stocks. Jean, on the other hand, brings a more lighthearted approach, viewing money as only worth the pleasure it can provide you. She prefers lots of stock and displays great interest in new ventures and other financial opportunities.

Of course, things really heated up when they talked about specific expenditures!

Every so often, Jean would get excited over the pleasant thought of purchasing a new piece of furniture for their house. Pete would quickly point out that by putting money into savings now they could afford more of this type of thing in the *future.* Jean would argue what a vast difference a new piece of furniture would make in the appearance and feel of their home *today.* "After all, what good is money if it doesn't bring you pleasure every now and then?" she maintained. "But solid, prudent planning for a secure and pleasurable retirement is important too," retorted Pete.

Their personality approaches came together like the clash of two shiny cymbals heard from miles away! Now we see why the temptation is so strong for these types to fall into "character assessments." While they seek support from their mate to live the "good life," it feels more like opposition! But is it really what it feels like? Healthy marriages do personality *assessments* first, delaying *judgments* about the other's character. They assume that differences are about personality, and that understanding leads to a successful mediation satisfying both parties.

How does this work? For example, is the issue of control about personality or character? And which one really has the better handle on the "good life," on being "fully alive"? Don't be too quick to judge!

First, let's take a closer look at two prominent pitfalls for journeyers: the "controller illusion" and the "half-alive illusion." Then we'll look at a common assessment struggle of the planner as he/she views a journeyer, which I call the "procrastination illusion."

The Controller Illusion

Indeed, *some* husbands are egotistical controllers with a fear-based, compulsive need to control, which is a character issue. But such is not the case with Pete, who simply has a strong preference for a planner approach to life. Pete feels most comfortable when life situations conform to his preconceived expectations. If your mate is a planner, *expect* him/her to start getting edgy when the anticipated situation appears to be nonconforming. He feels upset, not in the angry sense of the word, but in the "anxiety" sense. To live the "good life," preparation is key to anticipate uncomfortable situations that are avoidable. He is highly motivated to avoid the anxiety of chaos and surprise.

If he finds himself in uncomfortable situations that he considers could have been avoided, he may tend to put the blame on his soul mate. When Jean notes Pete's discomfort with the "chaos of change," the dreaded "C" word comes to her mind: he is a "controller"! (Maybe my mother was right about him, she wonders.) But Pete is just following his planner motivational bent, without malicious intent. He just isn't as comfortable, or as skilled as Jean is, in adapting and flexing with life's changing menus.

In fact, Pete is simply blinded to the benefits awaiting him in Jean's "lighter" approach to life...but not for long!

WHICH ONE IS HALF ALIVE?

Journeyers must beware of developing a kind of contempt for the planner's lifestyle of always trying to stay "in control." They can easily come to regard planners as half alive, living a narrow or limited existence. There is some degree of truth in this assessment, for planners do often miss the full experience of life in the "present" tense. What a shame, Jean says to herself, to have the feast of life spread before you and spend all day planning or worrying about the right way to approach it.

Consequently, the journeyer is far more comfortable with handling the unexpected. Jean is more casual about accidental incidents or little messes that may require masterful spontaneity and flexibility. If the bed is not perfectly made, it will not ruin her experience of the day. Her approach is to tackle it with a readiness for new experiences and relish adjusting to its wide array of variety.

If Pete allows Jean's personality motivation to rub off a little on him, he will relieve a lot of the self-generated stress in his life. When it comes to living in the present, Jean has the superior spirit, but when it comes to living in the future, Pete has a gift for Jean. What is it?

The Procrastination Illusion

Planners face a similar temptation of unwarranted "character assassination" in judging the motivation (or lack thereof!) of journeyers. Journeyers can easily be seen as "idlers" without direction, drifting their way through life. To planners, they can appear to be wasting a lot of valuable time because they lack serious goals. Moreover, getting started is difficult for journeyers. They are prone to indecision, waiting for more input, which appears to be procrastination.

For example, Pete complains in therapy that Jean tends to underappreciate his ability to anticipate and prepare for the future. Not only is he good at setting plans, but also he enjoys imagining their arrival. While he relishes a future weekend getaway or impending vacation trip, she delays getting too excited about it "until it really happens." This distresses him because he feels he is planning alone. Moreover, what excites him doesn't seem to move her at all.

If Jean lets some of Pete's personality motivation rub off on her, she can begin to get more things started—and finished! Moreover, she can begin to enjoy some of their jointly anticipated future plans—and savor them—in the present, rather than pushing them off into the numbing state of the "unknown future." And Pete can learn from Jean how to let go of the fight to try to manage life at the boundary of its unforeseen ragged edge, where he finds himself struggling to control the uncontrollable.

Let's look at some very practical ways to make the blending of a planner and journeyer foster more of the "good life" for each.

PRACTICAL RELATING FOR PLANNERS AND JOURNEYERS

The sailors were fighting for their lives that night, trying to keep their ship from capsizing in an English Channel snowstorm, when a strange thing happened. A stumpy, scruffy old passenger suddenly demanded to be lashed to the mast. He said he wanted to experience the sea's full fury so he could paint it.

To get him out of their way, they lashed him to the crow's nest. He stayed up there for hours, tossed by gale winds and drenched by snow and freezing salt water. And when British artist Joseph Turner got down, he painted the sea as no one ever had before! (*2500 Best Modern Illustrations,* Harper & Row Publishers, N.Y., 1935)

In marriage, empathy is a courageous act that exposes you to the potential "salt water" of your mate's suffering and pain, as well as his/her joys and pleasures. Such deepened understanding is priceless and irreplaceable! Empathy is the link that binds a couple inseparably as they walk through the storms and sunny days of life's journey together.

For journeyers and planners, consider the following practical suggestions as guides to begin the process of empathetic understanding of your opposite's world.

For a Planner Dealing with a Journeyer

Relational/Spiritual Principle 1   "Who of you by worrying can add a single hour to his life?" (Mt. 6:28)

Healthy *marital relating* is characterized by having expectations that are open to adjustments along the way.

Healthy *spirituality* is characterized by planning without worry.

Personality Principle 1   *Develop more comfort in going with the flow.*

Planners need to grow in their capacity to flex with changing events. They often waste energy trying to interpret or make situations conform to their preconceived mind-set. If you are a planner, you should note carefully and appreciatively the ability of your journeyer to temporarily get pushed off his/her plan—and remain cheerfully unstressed!

While every goal requires ignoring some side issues, planners may unconsciously put on blinders and miss many of life's experiences. They run the risk of "arriving" at some future goal, only to realize the emotional sacrifice made along the way of having reached the peak without enjoying the scenery along the way. *So develop more comfort in going with the flow.*

Relational/Spiritual Principle 2	"Is anything too wonderful for God?" Gen. 18:14
Personality Principle 2	*Embrace the present, including the positive aspects of surprise!*

Because they are prone to try to make their experience of the "flow" conform to their expectation, planners may overintellectualize the circumstantial pleasures that are handed to them. They are often receptive and open only to anticipated or "earned" pleasures. Because they view surprising joy or unmerited blessing as tangential, they too easily repress or blunt new experience that doesn't square with their disciplined lifestyle.

Consider surprises as life's way of bringing variety to you. Embrace surprise as welcome and perhaps wonderfully serendipitous. Unforeseen events will serve to call forth your underdeveloped capacity for creativity and resourcefulness. You can discover unused levels of intelligence and improvisational competence that were previously unknown. If you don't know what "improvisational competence" is, then just improvise and do the best you can in figuring it out.

This can prompt new feelings of pride, expansiveness, and self-confidence. You will be released from the disappointment of unmet expectations more often. You will have more energy to live in the present moment, with senses fully alive and abilities firing on all eight cylinders.

The constant postponement of present gratification can produce a person with low affect, appearing unable to embrace enthusiasm or passion for anything other than his/her narrow focus. Consider the elder brother in the parable of the prodigal son, who dutifully stayed home but apparently could not come to the party to celebrate his brother's arrival. He displays a sad inability to celebrate, to party, to let go and take in the joy of the occasion.

The unexpected occasion of great joy and feasting were not in his expected scenario. He is a conscientious plodder, a *planner,* and this bizarre ending does not fit into the belief system that he feels is the most appropriate approach to life. *You must learn to embrace the present, Mr. Planner, including the positive aspects of surprise!*

Relational/Spiritual Principle 3	"Blessed are the poor in spirit, for theirs is the kingdom of heaven." (Mt. 5:3)

Healthy *relating* is characterized by a light hold upon our opinions.

Healthy *spirituality* is characterized by a light hold on our will and a sincere openness to a higher will.

Personality Principle 3	*Consider persons with fixed opinions as half dead.*

Learn to go with the emotional goal that occasional changes of opinion represent strength. Flexing can mean adaptation to a better fit. Rigid mindsets can promote stress in terms of resisting inevitable change or working overtime to make the world conform to expectations. As a planner, make a mental option of a "Plan B" approach to your life: always being open to reexamination of your original opinion or choice.

In relating to your partner's different approach to life, beware of gaining a reputation as a self-centered controller with fixed positions. Are you only half aware of the changing environment around you? If someone asks for your opinion, give several alternatives, with the clear statement that they can decide for themselves. Are you able to state the strong points of view that oppose yours? State your opinion as one option rather than a foregone conclusion.

Relational/Spiritual Principle 4	Focus your energy on the problems in the *foreseeable* future, not in the *distant* future.

Personality Principle 4	*Don't get emotionally too far into the future (ahead of yourself).*

Thinking too far ahead can be destructive if it creates current anxiety. Learn to be faithful to tasks for today and tomorrow, and frame the *distant future* as a pleasant region beyond the boundaries of your current vision. Planners must beware of extrapolation of current negative facts and other automatic thinking patterns that thrust them *too far ahead*. These only serve to needlessly distract one from the required existential focus upon the present moment. They can depress one's mood and spirit unnecessarily.

Watch carefully how your journeyer deals with the distant future because journeyers *don't get emotionally too far into the future!*

For the Journeyer Dealing with a Planner

Relational/Spiritual Principle 1

"There is a time for everything, and a season for every activity under heaven: a time to be born and a time to die, a time to plant and a time to uproot ... " (Eccles. 3:1–2)

Wasting precious time comes as a result of not practicing the discipline of time management. This includes allocating time for planning.

Relational Principle 1

Growing in the essential skill of time management.

Planners are usually better at assessing and appreciating the appropriate length of time it takes to complete a task than journeyers. Time management always starts with answering the question of what needs to be done and in what order. Consider what rewards you would reap by completing a task. Then, compare those rewards with the consequences of putting it aside. This process makes it easier to see which goals have higher value.

The three fundamentals of time management are: (1) listing actions, (2) prioritizing actions, and (3) monitoring actions. For example, writing out plans on paper makes a seemingly elusive goal more concrete. In step two, prioritize the important versus the urgent, and learn to say "no" to more and more "unexpected emergencies." These are other-directed versus the self-directed plans that have the greatest value for you. Write out your priorities every morning (or the night before, to program your subconscious). Keep putting at the top of the list your "limiting step" or bottleneck that is most important to quickly and efficiently achieve your goal, and keep hammering away at getting that thing done.

In step three, visualize yourself taking the small steps that you need to accomplish your goal. Get a coach, or some way to monitor your progress, and reward yourself as you reach milestones. Remember, when your plan is done, your goal is half won. Visualization is a great way to get the planning process started.

A great result of time management is self-discipline, the essential key to self-esteem. Once we sense the lack of discipline within ourselves, it starts to erode our personhood. Journeyers must constantly deal with the temptation to ease up. When you give a little bit less than your best, you've started to decrease your self-esteem, the basic building block of the "good life." A little neglect can start as a small infection that can gradually grow into a lifestyle disease.

What's the antidote? All you have to do is *take action now!* Get started in *developing your skill at time management.*

Relational Principle 2	*Come to a deeper appreciation of building in consistent routines.*

Without a well-developed capacity for self-regimentation and purposeful discipline, journeyers are vulnerable to the winds of current fancy. Their aim to experience everything life has to offer can lead to a lack of productivity or wasted time. More time in your life to enjoy, explore, and coast actually comes from developing a consistent routine. Routines can breed efficiency and speed if handled properly. Busyness is not necessarily productivity.

For example, Jesus practiced the routine of prayer and self-care in order to carry out the long-term goal of achieving His Father's purpose. The Scriptures are full of passages about Jesus' habit of going into the hills on a regular basis to pray. He regularly did this before entering into his daily work. The discipline of solitude, submission, and other repetitive habits is often overlooked by journeyers (and other Western Christians), who sometimes mistake busyness for productivity.

Relational Principle 3	*Be more realistic in deadline planning and getting started.*

If you don't strike while the idea is hot and translate it into action fairly soon, the urgency starts to diminish. Journeyers know all too well that a month from now the passion is cold, and a year from now it is gone. Trust your intuitive wisdom and take action now, or otherwise your wisdom is wasted.

Here's the time to act: when the idea is hot and the emotion is strong! Let's say you want to change careers. First, take a night course. Go to the school and get all the information you can while the idea is hot and you are motivated. After the course is over, even if you decide to move to another career, you are wiser and further down the road than if you had done nothing.

Try to complete tasks a day or two *before* the deadline. Place a limit on information gathering and decision making. Look at the calendar year and ask yourself what three things you need to accomplish. Then schedule them in, planning backwards to ensure that you have allowed ample time—then add a bit more time.

The journeyer is typically poor at decisively setting a long-term goal and staying with it to completion. While drawn to things new and novel, he/she is easily distracted and can grow impatient with the conscientious plodding necessary for long-term project completion. Therefore, work with your planner mate in developing the ability to take action and complete tasks by enlisting him/her as your "accountability coach" to hold you on task. For example, journeyers need the help of a planner to do periodic "planning reviews" of their life direction and purpose. With appreciation, turn to your partner and say, "I admire your ability to plan ahead. I often succumb to the temptation to do one more thing, or get detoured off schedule." Planners are usually delighted to help with a rational review of the journeyer's investment of time and talent, particularly in terms of long-term productivity in the world. The planner might say, "Hey, by going 'one day at a time,' do you understand that you can go in circles and end up where you started?" To avoid falling prey to the temptation of the *"tyranny of the urgent"* as opposed to the *"commitment to the important,"* hire an accountability coach.

Where can you find such a coach or model person who maintains a strong commitment to long-term goal achievement? *Your partner!* Can you see how he or she can become God's helpmate, provided to you (free for the asking!) to develop your diminished capacity for a fully passionate and fulfilling style of life?

Why not reach for the highest and best lifestyle of all?

(Postscript: Our personality genius is given to us for a lifetime. This means that while a journeyer may never become a fully adept planner, journeyers can incorporate large degrees of planner proficiencies (and vice versa) into their own personality to expand it toward completeness. You will never have to worry about losing your natural personality traits—they will not be obliterated by emulating some of the beautiful qualities of your opposite!)

SCHEDULING, PLAY, AND THE "SPIRITUALITY" DIMENSION OF LIFESTYLE

"The glory of God is a person fully alive" is a long-held spiritual adage. How can each personality encourage another to embrace life to the fullest?

To be a whole person, you must maintain your ability to play because it is the only place where personality is afforded free, natural expression—it can exhale without inhibition. This means constantly fostering your own playful attitude toward life. Our deeply embedded "puritan" approach to American society has taught us for so long not to be playful that those natural tendencies within us have been repressed. But each personality motivation needs the opportunity to openly express itself without inhibition. This is afforded only in unfettered play, for joy is play's only intention.

When this intention is actually realized in joyful play, the time structure of the universe takes on a beautiful quality—namely, eternal. Eternal time is that spiritual state in which time ceases to matter. The activity at the moment is so engaging that the universe becomes timeless.

If a planner and journeyer keep play alive in their relationship long enough, it will become a way of life integral to the relationship. A healthy adult swings between two lifestyle polarities that need to be incorporated into every creature: serious work and lighthearted play, survival activity and joyful activity. Or another way of saying it: planning and journeying.

Play reorients hard-driving Americans to a higher rhythm of life that incorporates our spiritual dimension into our physical life. Everyone's spirit needs a periodic escape from the grit of life. Joyful play is a needed refueling of the spirit that is more natural and rewarding in the long run than other escapes (vacations, alcohol, TV, and the like). A balanced planner and journeyer couple will set aside a portion of each day for pursuits that have nothing to do with normal vocation. Among other things, play can disengage stressed out materialists (the extreme planner) from the spirit-draining pursuit of acquiring more things.

The capacity to play measures our spirituality. If you are a planner, ask yourself: Do I have enough *faith* to laugh, let go, and play during a stressful event? Can my spirit submit itself to alternatively engage and disengage from my current preoccupation? If I really believe in surrendering to a higher power, then shouldn't I live as if *"everything is beautiful in its time" (kairos)* and not be impatient with apparent delays?

For the journeyer, can I proactively plan into my weekly rhythm a pleasing cadence of work and play, productivity and pleasure? What is my answer to the deathbed question, "What did you accomplish with your life?"

SEXUAL JOY AS PLAY

Many planners and journeyers do not enjoy sex to its fullest potential. The usual problem is half-blind emotional architecture of their personality. The passionate respect for the mystery and "otherness" of one's partner can easily wane over time. Our *sexual personality differences* are another place where one wisely asks, "Do I need to change my attitude or approach toward my partner?" (see chapter 6 for your sexual preference guide).

For example, as we shall see in more detail in the final chapter, the planner will typically struggle with the *spontaneity required for sexual play.* He or she must accept this as an emotional/spiritual growth question. Can I expand beyond only anticipated sexual events and discomfort with sexual spontaneity, leading me to greater sexual passion and involvement with my mate? In practical terms, this may mean "going with the flow" of relaxing, lighter and longer foreplay to stretch him/her into a new dimension of enjoyable playfulness. The process of "playing toward greater intimacy" can move to a higher priority, making secondary his previous rush to get to the "goal" of sexual achievement.

On the other hand, the journeyer may struggle with being in the right mood for sexual play. He or she is typically more focused upon the present scene or mood and thus will be primarily guided by a sense of the current state of *what is appropriate at the moment.* The challenge for spiritual growth lays in developing a growing ability to sense what one's planning partner is anticipating for a given evening or weekend getaway. The planner may give signals of his/her desire for an anticipated coming sexual encounter that the journeyer will tend to minimize. When the signal is received, the challenge is to begin to slowly imagine, in the back of one's conscious mind, the coming moments of joy and fun that are already being imagined in the mind of the planner.

Our personality approach plays a *significant* and fascinating role in our sexual expression! It provides for interesting discussion in chapter 6.

SPIRITUAL PROFILES OF THE PLANNER AND JOURNEYER

The proverb is profoundly true that, at the deepest level, we are "spirits within a body." These profiles are intended as general definitions to aid in the process of pinpointing areas for potential spiritual growth. Remember: Personality preference and spiritual orientation do not always have a direct correlation. See if you can catch the general "spirit" of your lifestyle orientation and entertain suggestions where your "spirituality pathway" for future growth may lie.

The Planner as a Spiritual Profile

The disciplined and willful planner will be drawn to the God who is the Judge or Supreme Ruler. He will desire spiritual experience that fits into his systematic approach to life, much like the elder brother in the parable of the prodigal son. Heaven-on-Earth for the planner is to experience God's blessing through "arriving" or achieving a goal. He will take on mission projects that are concrete and require initiative. With his strong work ethic, the planner will choose to burn out rather than rust out.

The cross that planners will naturally tend to avoid or be blinded to is the joy of spontaneous, existential, in-the-moment living. Their awareness of all their senses is often blunted by their goal orientation. They are frequently neglectful of the serendipitous side of life, with the surprising graces and comforts of God going underappreciated.

Because a planner dislikes disorder and helplessness, he may not be able to pray or play like a child. He will not enjoy fully the pleasures of grace and unmerited love of God due to his propensity to earn things or "make things happen" by virtue of his effort. He may be prone to perfectionism, rigidity, or self-righteousness. These attributes can possibly stem from his discriminating, Pharisee-like orientation toward top-level competence or achievement in any realm, including spirituality. If highly spiritually motivated, the planner will have to watch out for occasional spiritual dryness that comes from inability to appropriate grace.

In general, for the planner to achieve robust, passionate spiritual wholeness, he will have to learn to ease away from his keen desire for self-driven, goal-oriented production. He needs to grow in his ability to be more receptive to, and grab hold of, God's surprises and pleasures in the present moment.

The Journeyer as a Spiritual Profile

The journeyer will tend to be drawn to the God of the process, who brings of-the-moment redemption and healing in spontaneous response to human predicaments. God often speaks to the journeyer through unexpected changes, surprises, and small gestures of unforeseen provision. The journeyer is very ready to receive God's grace, possessing an easy acceptance of current circumstance, as the state of "being" is a more important priority than the state of "doing." Heaven-on-Earth is a spontaneous happening of good times, perhaps lighthearted joy and playfulness, as an awareness of God's graceful and sometimes mysteriously rewarding presence.

The "cross of discomfort" (and spiritual growth) for the journeyer is found in two areas. The first is seizing choice, the personal power that gives you the advantage over your feelings and fate. Painful choices mean taking responsibility and action, realizing that your life belongs to you and you alone. Journeyers can take action by owning the painful responsibility that their present as well as future life is all about "choice."

The second is fostering a consistent regimentation toward the end of *implementing the long-term goals of their lives.* Setting long-term goal deadlines is often the key to getting the journeyer into motion in this area. The discipline of a systematic or well-ordered lifestyle is difficult for the journeyer, who tends to feel confined by the regimentation of the inner or outer spiritual disciplines.

In general, the journeyer needs to take more responsibility for ordering his/her life. Procrastination and impulsiveness need to be set aside in favor of disciplines that will yield greater spiritual productivity and consistency.

The Concluding Tale of Two Approaches: A Financial Merger

To discuss their differing approaches to money, Pete and Jean visited a financial planner, who took a page right out of my book, metaphorically speaking. He suggested that a solid financial plan would incorporate both approaches, with a broad-based portfolio that would provide both security in volatile periods (Pete's conservative approach) and upside potential in bullish times (Jean's more aggressive approach).

I suggested to Pete and Jean that, metaphorically speaking, their relationship appreciation portfolio needed broadening as well. Indeed, compromise is not a dirty word in marriage relationships—but to the contrary, a key element of marital bliss. Incorporation of the other's proficiency into their own, to the greatest extent possible, only serves to make them broader and more appreciative of overlooked good things in life.

I gave them the following assignment. Jean was to take pride in the growing savings account. She was to join Pete in watching over its growth, verbally affirming, on a periodic basis, her envisioned pleasures of "great future days" together. This meant that she would have to occasionally say "no" to a current expenditure in order to save and say "yes" for an even better day in the future. But why not *enjoy a little more of the future* that Pete already enjoys (in his mind) by talking about it and savoring it as if it were happening today?

I suggested to Pete that he budget to periodically buy a brand new piece of furniture. When the new piece arrived, he was to find ways to absolutely fall in love with that piece of furniture—and what it represented to Jean. The joy of newness, the glory of a change of scenery, the enhancement of the room setting, the comfort of the cushions, and so on. In other words, he was to enjoy the immediate pleasures of the moment that planners have a tendency to minimize—and miss out on! In other words, Jean's joy in the piece of furniture was to find equal or exceeding joy in him! Why let her have all the fun?

Your life can get bigger and better if you will occasionally mount the courage to try on the strangely wonderful lifestyle approach of our opposite. Trust me, it works!

Chapter 4

ENERGY SOURCES: THE "LET'S STAY HOME—NO, LET'S GO OUT" LEISURE CONFLICT

Ralph and Amy have a problem: they derive energy from diametrically opposite sources! I call Amy the *activator* type because she thrives in the world of *active* social participation. She finds the idea of socializing an energizing thought. Ralph, on the other hand, is the *reflector* type, whose natural inclination is to find replenishment in a solitary pursuit like *reflection*. He finds the idea of socializing a draining thought, preferring instead the quiet solitude of home.

Amy, the activator, makes the usual complaints about Ralph, the reflector:

1. "He doesn't like to socialize. He would rather stay home, read, or watch TV."
2. "In social settings, he is either very quiet, or makes tactless, opinionated statements."
3. "I wonder what other people think when he displays no enthusiasm. It's as if it's almost embarrassing."

Ralph, the reflector, makes the usual complaints about Amy, the activator:

1. "She doesn't like to sit still and relax. She's always on the run."
2. "In social settings, sometimes she makes embarrassing shallow remarks."
3. "She is so quick to jump enthusiastically into social affairs. I wonder if she is running away from introspection, some hidden feelings—or me."

Just as we need to replenish our bodies with food and rest, the motivational batteries of our psyche and spirit require restoration as well. Our inner person will inexorably gravitate to a place where, apart from daily demands, it can choose the kind of activity that nourishes it. Every couple must jointly carve out this important "place," clearly understanding and empowering the other to do what he/she yearns to do in their prized free time. When what *sustains* one partner actually *depletes* the other, you've got an "energy incompatibility" problem that needs to be addressed before it becomes a major source of irritation!

Like the irritating grain of sand that churns along and eventually brings down the entire cliff, energy incompatibility for Ralph and Amy was a nagging cause of emotional displacement. Each blamed the other, overtly or covertly, as being "a ball and chain" standing in the way of "what I love to do." I will show you how they paradoxically turned their grain of sand into a "pearl" of personal growth! (We reflector types love to play with paradoxes and metaphors!)

THE ENERGY SOURCES OF THE ACTIVATOR AND REFLECTOR

In the world of psyche replenishment, persons are generally drawn toward one of two sources. They are either pulled toward the *external* world of connection with people or the *inner* world of connection with self. Like homing pigeons under the power of natural instinct, we will find ourselves lured toward one or the other.

Activator	*Reflector*
finds nourishment in interaction with others from others	finds nourishment in retreat
drained by introspection	stimulated by introspection
prefers being in motion, participating, or acting in concert with others	prefers sedentary activities and solitary pursuits rather than group activity
finds it easy to conform and engage others in an interactive social setting	finds it draining to conform and engage others in an interactive social setting
outer focus results in being energized by comments or feedback of belonging, being with, or approval from others	inner focus results in being energized by stimulation of reflection, self-integration, and self-soothing without feedback of others

Characteristic Behaviors:

Activator

energized, quick, ready to go into action when called

often inept at objectifying or stepping outside of an activity in order to evaluate it

enjoys watching or hearing thoughtful discourse or informative dialogue as an interested spectator

can easily adapt mood to fit social occasion (This may be viewed as phony or "acting" by a reflector.)

Reflection on spirituality or philosophical issues is not typically of intense interest.

Reflector

calculating, ponderous, slow to go into action when called

adept at objectifying or stepping outside of an activity in order to ponder or evaluate it

enjoys engagement in thoughtful discourse or informative dialogue as an interested participant

has difficulty changing mood to fit social occasion (Can be sarcastic if feeling coerced into an uncomfortable setting.)

Reflection on spirituality or philosophical issues can often be of intense interest.

Two Different Approaches to Socializing:

Activator

Social setting tension—partner may create embarrassment by conveying to others:

a lack of interest in them *(Why doesn't he say something to convey an interest?)*

snobbishness, aloofness *(They may think he feels superior to them.)*

overly withdrawn or social ineptness *(He appears to be a misfit or nerd.)*

insensitive, inappropriate, or tactless remarks *(He has no sensitivity toward offending feelings or beliefs of others. For example:*

On the telephone, he has the manners and monotone of a caveman. He is clueless when it comes to warmth or empathy. He seems unaware of how he is coming across to others.)

would never leave a party too early *(Unless he was rude and embarrassing.)*

Reflector

Social setting tension—partner may create embarrassment by conveying to others:

an intense interest in them or overfriendliness *(Why is she acting so friendly with him?)*

inane or thoughtless remarks *(They might think she is stupid.)*

shallow understanding of a conversation *(She appears to grasp little about the topic.)*

fearfulness of rejection or oversensitivity to social correctness and conformity *(She has no sensitivity toward integrity and only cares about fitting in with others. For example:*

Like a chameleon, she can talk in a sweet tone on the phone, hang up, and blast me without missing a beat. She is clueless in regard to authenticity and congruence. She acts like a different person in different circumstances.)

Always ready to leave a party early *(She could spend the night chitchatting.)*

Marital Relationship Implications:

Activator	*Reflector*
May feel constrained or limited by a reclusive or socially stoic spouse. May require social needs met in activities without partner that satisfy psyche or relationship urges, for example, women's group activity, community group, bridge group, church, and so on.	May build boundaries or walls to avoid intrusions upon his/her psychic reenergizing time. For example, time to watch TV (football can be a "place" fitting for replenishment), work in the garage, time on computer, reading, study, and the like. All offer solitude or low demand to conform socially.

The *Charis* or Gift of Each Personality

Each personality offers a gift or way of enhancing our lives. The Greek word *charis,* from which we derive our word "charismatic," means grace. These little powers of enhancement can be called the *charis* or grace found within each person, as they are God-endowed delights that benefit our lives. As we have seen, *charis* is appropriately applied to each personality's attributes as cherishable qualities to be affirmed and appreciated. Indeed, each of us is a charismatic personality, if our mate chooses to focus on our endowments and not our weaknesses!

Let's see if we can discover some of the hidden treasures offered to the world through the beautiful *charis* or graces found in activators and reflectors.

Activators	*Reflectors*
unload emotions as they go *(Don't consider them shallow: they are present, accessible, and this is a healthy quality that reflectors need to develop!)*	control their emotions and tend to protect them, even when intense *(Don't consider them emotionless: they can be very passionate once the cap on the bottle is unleashed!)*
are relational persons with concern for decency, community, and helping make the social world in which people live more comfortable	are thinking persons of ideas, culture, and reason, who gain energy from reflection upon history, varying perspectives, and conceptual novelty
can invest themselves fully in the activities they focus upon or throw themselves into	tend to be reserved, with measured responsiveness to people and events until they have had time to reflect upon them
are often cooperative, participative, likable, and well regarded	often honor commitments once they overcome reservations to commit

Emotional Intelligence (EQ):

EQ Activators	*EQ Reflectors*
high emotional intelligence in interpersonal world with others, and lower in intrapersonal world (introspection)	high emotional intelligence in intrapersonal world (introspection) and lower in interaction with others

The New World Offered to Activators through Reflectors

In Ray Bradbury's introduction to *Dandelion Wine,* he makes the citizens either gods or midgets. The midgets walked tall so as not to embarrass the gods, and the gods crouched so as to make the small ones feel at home. Isn't that what life is all about—the ability to go around back and come up inside other people's heads and look out at the miracle and say, "Oh, so *that's* how you see it!"

Practice the kenosis principle by entering into your reflector's frame of reference. You can do this (for a time) by making the effort to "see" and experience the world as your partner does. In each section, sense your own half-blindness as you find yourself saying, "Oh, so *that's* how you see it!"

Relational/Spiritual Principle 1	"For which one of you, when he wants to build a tower, does not sit down first and calculate the cost, to see if he has enough to complete it? Otherwise, when he has laid a foundation, and is not able to finish, all who observe it begin to ridicule him." (Luke 14:28–29)

Periodic *reflection* upon the direction and quality of one's life is essential to healthy spirituality. Shallow, foolish decisions are often based upon initial enthusiasm alone, without appropriate *reflection.*

Relational Principle 1	*Pause frequently to evaluate the results of your activity.*

"The unexamined life is not worth living," said a wise philosopher. Yet such wisdom is lost on many activators, whose lives are often lived in a numbing whirl of motion. In their desire to find life in activity, activators often cheat themselves of the fruits of the enriching perspective that comes only through contemplation.

Activators need to see themselves as quite adept at *doing* and usually inept at *being*. These two approaches to energizing one's life are illustrated in the two sisters in the biblical story of Mary (the reflector) and Martha (the activator). When Jesus came to their house for a visit, hospitable Martha became preoccupied in *doing* "many things." On the other hand, Mary was delighted in *being* in the presence of Jesus, and simply "sat at his feet" to soak up the special moment. Observing the differing approaches, Jesus said to the harried Martha, "Mary has chosen the better part."

Martha probably didn't get it. In psychotherapy, I often encounter activators with dulled skills of introspection, viewing the process as the meaningless equivalent to "contemplating one's navel." Yet, their busy, hectic lives are often not as fulfilling or rewarding as they could be, including their marriages. This is because they are stuck in a superficial routine of activity and have grown accustomed to burying the experience of their deeper feelings and thoughts.

If suppressed over a lengthy period of time, like any other ability, the gift of awareness and accessibility to the deeper level of life is diminished or lost. Superficial experience of their inner self is their imprisoning "life sentence"—and high-speed activators can "sentence" themselves without even knowing it!

Amy admitted that, like many activators, she can get into a rut at times, going through a repetitive cycle of activities over and over, without a sense of well-being or newness. I pointed out the proverb: "a rut is a grave with the ends knocked out!" She asked, "Okay, then how can activators find renewal in the midst of their many activities?"

I suggested to her that creative people are always hungry for new knowledge and information, even on seemingly unrelated subjects. Because knowledge contributes to the process of creativity, I suggested she consider developing her skill of *introspection* as her new area of *knowledge acquisition.*

For example, in the process of creativity, there is typically an incubation stage in which a new insight or idea is allowed to sit in the back of your brain and "stew." For activators, introspection can mean learning how to let an issue percolate, patiently setting it aside without immediate action. This process is like a farmer planting seed and then *patiently waiting* for the rain, or a baker mixing bread but *patiently waiting* for it to rise. Pay attention all activators: it will not work if you try to force or speed up the process! The potential for creative forces to work on you and in you will be short-circuited! You must give your inner self the gift of time: let it work on your issue, feelings, or idea. Be patient, go deeper, let it stew—and believe that a future *eureka* moment will come.

Like many couples I see, Amy and Ralph had stopped talking about what was going on in the deeper places in their lives. I suggested that every Sunday on the way home from church they discuss how the theme of the service or sermon impacted each of them emotionally and spiritually. They were missing the stimulation of discussion and integration of more profound values or alternative approaches that could enrich their lives. Ralph's reserved and questioning attitude toward certain issues (deeper or more complex than Amy appreciated) needed to be taken seriously by Amy.

For example, if you are an activator with a business problem, one potential creative solution is to try the contrarian approach. Seek out a vendor, a competitor, or a customer to interview, and listen for information that you would never have come up with yourself.

If you are an activator married to a reflector, you have built-in accessibility to the contrarian approach of a more *introspective* person! Appreciate your mate's approach for its potential of opening new areas of creativity and renewal that you would have never seen for yourself! Make your focus of attention for next year a more powerful development of the joyous skill of *introspection.* Work at getting better at *being* as opposed to always *doing.*

Relational/Spiritual Principle 2	"Be still and know that I am God." (Psalm 46:10)

Healthy spirituality requires periodic introspection into the quality of care being given to one's inner person. Introspection brings direct results because self-care is the basis of all quality caring of others.

Relational Principle 2	*Pause frequently to know yourself better.*

The first step in building a vital connection with your soul mate is for you to become a soul yourself. A soul is an authentic, real individual with concrete, identifiable needs, and stoic denial of one's needs or dreams has a deadening effect on a relationship. Activators are prone to procrastinate or set aside attentiveness to inner needs, becoming lost souls in terms of genuine self-awareness.

On vacation after a busy season, I find it often takes two or three days for me to adjust to the new dimension of being in rare intimacy with my inner person. When our bodies and minds are stressed by hectic activity, we starve ourselves of many things, including the relaxation that leads to creative insight into our fears and hopes. As pastor Eugene Peterson put it in an article to pastors,

> The word busy is the symptom not of commitment but of betrayal. I know it takes time to develop a life of prayer: set-aside, disciplined, deliberate time. It isn't accomplished on the run...I know I can't be busy and pray at the same time. I can be active and pray, but I cannot be busy and pray. I cannot be inwardly rushed, distracted, or dispersed. In order to pray I have to be paying more attention to God than to what people are saying to me.

Spiritual writer Ann Wells tells of her brother's remark upon finding a "special silk lingerie" in his deceased wife's drawer as they prepared for her memorial service. "She bought this 8 years ago for a 'special occasion,' and she never wore it." He slammed the drawer shut and said, "Ann, don't ever save anything for a 'special occasion.' Every day you are alive is a 'special occasion.'"

As she reflected on those words, her life changed. She began to look at her daily activities from a different perspective, pondering the deeper meaning to her experience. She began to dust less and read more. She sat on the deck admiring the view rather than fussing about the weeds in the garden. Instead of saving good perfume for "special occasions," she wore it so store clerks could enjoy its scent. From her new perspective, she determined that from then on, her life should be a pattern of experience to savor, not just to endure. It became infinitely richer because she was no longer saving anything for a "special occasion."

This story illustrates the power of reflection that is easily overlooked by activators. With their natural bent toward "what people are saying or doing," activators can easily minimize getting in touch with self and God. Learn the value of pause, of giving yourself time to "see" and "feel" an issue from several perspectives. Wait until you become centered or grounded in how *you* want to respond to it. Ask yourself "why" more often. Why am I doing this? Believe me, there's an answer to every why.

Learn the value of the pause to take a longer, deeper look. One of its more delicious fruits is to periodically *pause to better know yourself.*

Relational/Spiritual Principle 3	"Do not be conformed to this world..." (Romans 12:1)
Relational Principle 3	*In social settings, beware of conformity or "people pleasing" leading to intellectual or emotional superficiality.*

Activators can depend too highly on the excitement generated by the given social setting. They can be vulnerable to the temptation of desiring to hear words of approval or praise from others for their appearance, conduct, or even the energy they bring to family or social gatherings. This adept proficiency in harmonizing with a particular setting in a winsome way is a strength that can become a weakness if the activator loses his/her sense of individuality or self-awareness. Because of an activator's bent to focus primarily on the perceptions of others around them, they can develop a fluctuating self-view or become selfless chameleons without a genuine presence that marks them as authentic. The ability to become the life of the party can work to the activator's detriment when the party is over and it is time to focus on the serious needs or deficiencies within his/her life.

In short, while reflectors tend to be more proficient at being serious, sober, and grave, activators tend to be more proficient at being fun, jocular, and light. When it is time for serious introspection, activators can learn much from the skills of reflector types. Integrating a more profound ability to introspect will only serve to deepen and enrich the active life of an activator.

Summary for activator coupled with reflector:

1. Pause frequently to evaluate direction.
2. Pause frequently to know yourself better.
3. In social settings, beware of conformity or people pleasing, which sometimes leads to intellectual or emotional superficiality,

Amy's Opportunity to Grow through Ralph

Before: "A lot of the time I don't know what he's thinking. But I can tell he is pondering or reflecting upon something. It frustrates me."

Now: "I need to allocate more time for my inner person, and listen to 'messages from base' coming from within. I should slow down and take the time to find out what he is thinking about. If he won't open up to me, I'll take the lead in opening up to him, and believe that eventually he will, in like fashion, open up to me. At any rate, it is the better approach anyway to share one's musings and issues than to just hold it in. Being a little introspective or philosophical from time to time can be fun, and actually be rewarding as well in terms of making us more intimate, even if we disagree."

Before: "He doesn't like to socialize. He would rather read or sit at home. He is such a social deadbeat. I feel like I'm a prisoner because he doesn't want to do so many fun things I would like to do."

Now: "Negotiating a good balance of going out and staying home is critical for both of us if we are going to be happy and learn from each other. He needs to get out more, and I may need to stay in more. This is a great topic for the emotional and spiritual growth of both of us. We can help each other to grow with small nudges and a shared commitment to listen to the other when we conflict over our 'free time' activity choices."

Before: "He is so cautious about jumping in and trying new experiences."

Now: "I need to grow more skilled in counting the costs before I make commitments that I can't keep or that I'm sorry I made."

Before: "I never paid any attention to how superficial I sounded at a social gathering. Who cares?"

Now: "I came to realize that this was Ralph's rationalization about some of his tactless remarks at family gatherings or work: who cares? From another's perspective, being superficial may be as bad as being tactless. I decided that I want to continue to have fun but to be more aware of being serious or intellectually sincere at the appropriate time as well."

The New World Offered to Reflectors through Activators

Relational/Spiritual Principle 1

"Behold, I stand at the door and knock. If any one hears my voice and opens the door, I will come in and eat with him. He who conquers, I will grant that he sit down on my throne, as I myself conquered." (Rev. 3:20–21)

The peace of spiritual serenity only comes through a total, passionate commitment.

That depth of commitment calls one to surrender all rationalization, and go *toward* the pain or *through* the pain, rather than intellectualizing it.

Relational Principle 1

Invest more passion and engagement in humanity.

The reflector's deliberate, cautious tendency can keep him on the sidelines of life. If he will only observe and listen, the voice of God calling him to "give himself away" to some cause is coming through his partner. How? In his partner's example of impassioned, active engagement in some cause or activity involves shared humanity. The inclination to ponder and sit on the sidelines of the agony and ecstasy of the human fray can render the reflector half alive, living blind to the benefits of a full commitment or of fearlessly giving of himself without reservation.

As Oliver Wendell Holmes put it, "I find the great thing in this world is not so much where we stand as in what direction we are moving. To reach the port of heaven, we must sometimes sail with the wind and sometimes against it—but we must sail, not drift, nor lie at anchor." The reflector's proficiency in testing the direction of the wind can subject him to the fearful world of reservation rather than total commitment to his cause.

This is especially true, for example, of the novel upcoming adventure planned enthusiastically by his partner if it contains a great deal of interaction with people and activity, which he is inclined to desperately avoid. Nevertheless, these social demands that tend to drain him are his point of personal growth. His abstract world of reflective ideas needs to be challenged and tested. His reflection becomes eccentric or impractical when it is not brought under scrutiny to prove its relevant effectiveness.

Relational/Spiritual Principle 2	"God has set eternity in the hearts of men, yet so that man will not find out the work which God has done from the beginning even to the end. For there is nothing better for men than to be happy and do good while they live." (Eccles. 3:11–12)

Healthy spiritual persons act within the limitations of their boundaries.

Reflectors can become paralyzed by their fore-thinking tendency to require full understanding before risking participation.

Relational Principle 2	*Have fewer reservations based upon being comfortable first.*

Reflectors often rationalize their tendency to stand on the sidelines of active participation in social or community involvement. They frequently complain of a lack of full understanding, which is used to justify their reclusive or nonparticipative behavior. This discomfort is often encountered in dialogue with their partners, who would like to see them join more wholeheartedly in social activities. It is at this very point of discomfort where the call of life is to be heard. It is here where the reflector must hear the call to move toward his pain and thereby end it. In his half blindness, he fails to see the potential that these experiences with people hold for him.

Over a period of time, interaction with people broadens our empathy and compassion for the ethos and pathos of our shared humanity. We were created for relationship. As respected German theologian Karl Barth stated, "humanity out of relationship with humanity is inhumanity."

As we learn to share in the common lives of fellow humans, we grow in our appreciation of the heights and depths of human souls. Becoming more aware of our interconnection with all humanity, we develop greater passion for the breadth and diversity of life, including the full embrace of its slings and arrows of outrageous fortune.

This also applies to spiritual exploration. To protect his/her inner comfort, the reflector often will employ the classic defense of preunderstanding *before* fully investing himself in an investigation of spiritual issues. By closing off possible experience of the spiritual dimension, he shuts out new realms of existence and perspective. He will remain spiritually dead, for spiritual quests must, of necessity, demand the investment of one's full spirit—or else the exploration is counterfeit. As has been said, one cannot cross a large chasm in small jumps. This applies to the spiritual experience, which requires a real investment of trust, called by philosopher Soren Kirkegaard the "leap of faith." Real investigation requires opening one's heart to some consequence as a result of making a transfer of trust.

For the timid reflector, the spiritual dimension holds great promise as a potential gold mine of inner peace and satisfaction—*if* he would heed its daring call. That call may well be heard through deepened admiration for the adventuresome—if sometimes reckless abandon—of his activator partner!

Precisely because the reflector may be tempted to take the quieter path, he needs the encouragement that comes through being connected in heart and soul to a character like the fellow in one of author Alan Paton's South African novels. Talking of going to heaven, he said, "When I go up there, which is my intention, the Big Judge will say, 'Where are your wounds?' And if I say I haven't any, He will say, 'Was there nothing to fight for?' I could not face that question."

It is wonderful fuel for the flickering fire of any fainthearted reflector to be around such passionately committed persons, who would rather die for their cause than live for their self.

Relational Principle 3   *In social settings, practice participating and "being present" rather than being a spectator.*

For reflectors, going toward "the pain that produces gain" means learning to be more comfortable in social settings. The cold demeanor and rigid body language of the typical "highly guarded" reflector can communicate a diversity of different messages—most of them negative. How do you like the challenge of relating to a person with a cold demeanor and rigid, frozen appearance? Watch a quiet person at a social gathering, and see if the message you get is positive or negative. In most cases, silence produces distance, as others will react to silence as an ominous, negative signal.

The next time you are in a social setting, check out your level of involvement. At the minimum, try to let your body language express some interest in what is being said or done. Better, try to make simple, honest statements or ask questions that convey interest in someone else. In other words, get the focus off of your own awkwardness or discomfort. Most importantly, *get involved in the activity.* Practice empathy as one human being relating to another, one person at a time, and find yourself starting to be more natural.

The reflector should consider each social occasion an opportunity to practice being "present," the psychological term to describe a person who is authentic and congruent, without pretense. He has no outer "shell" or defense mechanism of processing social interactions through an intellectual or emotional "comfort screen." This person is "present" because he has ready access to his thoughts or feelings, with hardly a difference between his *inner* and *outer* person.

A good test of being "present" is to first take a deep breath and relax. Second, see how readily you can make an "I" statement, such as: (1) "I am feeling...", (2) "I am thinking...", or (3) "I would like..." Try this "present" test the next time you are at a social gathering.

Self-development in the social sphere will not only produce greater enjoyment of such settings—but will also bring joy to your activator mate! Make next year's "growth resolution" a resolve to relax, *participate, and be present in each social setting,* transforming the discomfort of its initial pain into your gain!

Summary for reflector coupled with activator:

1. Consider more involvement in shared humanity.

2. Have fewer reservations based upon being comfortable first.

3. In social settings, practice participating and being present rather than being a "spectator."

Growth Areas for Ralph Seen through Amy

Before: "She is shallow and often naïve."

Now: "I need to enjoy people more. Instead of simply observing or judging, I need to get more involved with people socially."

Before: "She is always socializing and 'on-the-run.' "

Now: "I'm impressed with the way she gets passionately involved in activities or with people."

Before: "She doesn't think before she speaks."

Now: "I need to be more skilled and at ease in expressing my inner person."

SPIRITUAL PROFILES

The Activator as a Spiritual Type

The activator will tend to be drawn to the God who enjoins us to actively build and participate in community. It will be an active God (e.g., Healer, Sustainer) who values people who are *doing* things. God will be expected to show up through revelations in the unfolding drama of life as found in experience with people and events in the world. Heaven-on-Earth for the activator is staying busy and participating with others.

The "cross of discomfort" (and spiritual growth) is found in the agony of solitude, meditation, and introspection. It is hard for an activator to sit still. The loneliness of feeling left out or detached from others yields a "dark night of the soul" that is excruciating for activators.

For example, if they are Christians, they like to focus on the people-centered activities of Christ, and tend to neglect his almost daily ritual of quiet meditation in the early morning. As activators follow their natural tendency to focus upon the "real world" of people and things, it becomes easy to neglect carving out quiet times to hear the voice of God coming through the "inner world" of their "self"—their thoughts and feelings.

Pause frequently to listen to "messages from base," that is, your body or your innermost spirit. Are you getting fatigued or burned out? Instead of living a reactionary lifestyle, always responding to demands from outside yourself, consider forging a more blended approach that incorporates your needs as well as others. (A totally outside-in lifestyle will inevitably lead to burnout.) In this new lifestyle of more frequent pause, develop more skill in listening intently to the "still small voice" of God speaking within. That means moving into action as a result of hearing one's inner voices and more carefully considering them as messages from God.

In general, for spiritual completeness, the activator will be required to practice more awareness and activity in the inner disciplines. For example, this could mean practicing the personal inspiration of quiet reflection, private prayer, and allocating more space for self-discovery.

The Reflector as a Spiritual Type

The reflector will have a tendency to be drawn to the God of individual experience. The identity of God and self will be important to the reflector, who will be in search of a God who helps a person transcend the unpleasant experiences of the outer world. Heaven-on-Earth is the comfortable experience of God speaking in a quiet, deeply individual way to His beloved child.

The "cross of discomfort" for the reflector is found in doing something about the distressful outer world that intrudes upon his/her inner serenity. While tempted to withdraw into the preferred independent world, the reflector needs to push out into interaction with others—probably more than he knows. If he doesn't, he can eventually become a useless recluse or an eccentric who is out of touch with reality.

In general, for spiritual completeness, the reflector needs social interaction and a more passionate level of service and participation in the struggles of the "human community."

Chapter 5

BELIEF SYSTEMS: THE SKEPTIC AND THE DREAMER DILEMMA

THE SET OF THE SAIL

I said to one who sailed the sea
That it surely was a marvel to me,
How ships go out on their golden quest
And ever the wind blow out of the West?

The sailor smiled as he answered me,
"Go where you will if you're on the sea,
It matters not what winds prevail—
For all depends on the set of the sail."

—Anonymous

Rod and Hillary have a perplexingly different "set of the sail" when it comes to belief systems. They pose the question uttered by countless couples: *How can persons with such different belief systems ever mesh their lives to find mutual happiness?*

Hillary, an *envisioner*, lamented the typical complaints about her *examiner* mate:

1. "He is such a cautious skeptic, stuck in the same old safe beliefs and routines."
2. "Why can't he be open to new possibilities, a little imagination, a passionate dream?"

3. "Why doesn't he have just a little interest in the spiritual realm—which he knows is so meaningful to me?"

Rod, an *examiner,* reported the typical complaints about his *envisioner* mate:

1. "She is so easily excited about new possibilities—that could be illusions."
2. "Why isn't she more curious about facts or evidence for her beliefs?"
3. "Why is she so enthusiastic about the spiritual world, which often lacks grounding in scientific fact or hard reality?"

THE PERCEPTION FILTER OF THE SKEPTIC AND THE DREAMER

We can't help it. We are not even aware of it.

It is our perception filter, the intriguing way we attend to certain kinds of data and ignore others. This pull toward particular kinds of data has a big influence on our beliefs, since there is a skeptic and dreamer filter inside all of us. We will be pulled or prejudiced more than we care to admit by the self-reinforcing observations generated by the loop of our perception filter! The loop works this way: *what we expect to observe, we observe; and what we expect tends to be conformed to previous observation!*

The filter found in our particular personality approach keenly effects what we *expect to observe.* These expected observations play a critical role in the formation of our beliefs, as diagrammed below.

The Examiner Filter	*Belief System*
Its preference for objective, verifiable data tends to lead to	trust in conventional, proven approaches (science, rationality, etc.) or established, traditional religious practice or beliefs. May question or take an agnostic/"doubting Thomas" position or play "devil's advocate."

Envisioner Filter	*Belief System*
Its preference for subjective, inner data tends to lead to	trust in innovative business/personal ideas or visionary secular/religious movements (such as creative/progressive churches, innovative praise or healing movements, and intuitive feelings). Often trust in breakthrough personal, subjective spiritual experiences (being "born again," miraculous gifts, etc.).

If you are an examiner like Rod and I, you prefer data you can "get your hands on." It is the kind of information that is scientific, tangible, proven in history, or verifiable in some way other than just one person's inner experience. This kind of information seems more "real" and trustworthy than the uncertainty of the new and untried world of potential experiences. In my marriage, I am more cautious and skeptical than my wife, Helen, preferring conventional or established belief systems as proven by some track record. No, you won't find Ron buying oceanfront property in Iowa!

What happens when my belief system rubs up against my envisioner mate Helen's, as she loves to consider new things? Being a "seer," who observes life as full of possibilities and fresh visions, she is quite comfortable with the notion that life offers better prospects than what simply meets the eye. She is sorely tempted to become frustrated with my "doubting Thomas" tendency to hold onto the same patterns: "What a dull old stick in the mud!" (And, as an examiner, I can't believe how quickly she can readily switch to another approach without a great deal of concern for "checking it out"!)

See if you can find yourself and your mate in one of the following generalized approaches:

THE EXAMINER AND ENVISIONER APPROACHES

The Skeptical Examiner	*The "Seer" Envisioner*
most comfortable with tangible, verifiable data or information	quite comfortable with data that exists in the realm of possibility
rests in solid, grounded "truth" as most foundational, trustworthy, and believable	drawn toward exciting, imaginative "truth" as most attractive, motivational, and believable
feels secure in established patterns and conventional ways of doing or thinking about things	feels limited by established patterns or strictly conventional ways of doing or thinking about things
If Examiner Is a Reasoner *(Decision Maker)*	*If Envisioner Is a Relater* *(Decision Maker)*
Tends to believe others as possibly wrong. Prone to taking a questioning or skeptical position of neutrality or *disbelief* in the positive attributes or promises of others. Concern is: do attributes fit evidence as found in past *history* of the person?	Tends to believe others as probably right. Prone to taking an unquestioning or naïve position of support or *belief* in the positive attributes or promises made by others. Concern is: do attributes conform to their vision or generalized *sense* of the person?

May convey negativity or skepticism toward others who are trying to change their ways or have "changed their mind" and have a new belief.	May be poor observers of others' behaviors that would be negative or contrary to preferred "vision" of that person.

Cherishing Factors

Examiner	*Envisioner*
"Solid as the Rock of Gibraltar,"—is the dogged, plodding type.	"Imagination rules the world," said the motivational leader Napoleon.
Long-suffering, prefers moderation in all things, savors contentment and having things settled and conventional. Cherish this consistent integrity of belief.	Romantic, the music makers of life, savors the prospects of joyous rapture, for example, a blossoming rose or a new adventure. Cherish this spiritual thirst for life.
Great investigator, problem-solving detective who analyzes current data and finds solutions: Appreciate around the house with problematic situations and solutions.	Great with instinctive knowledge, amazing inner insights, and sixth sense of the inward eye: Appreciate energy and instinct for "good things" that lay ahead.
Wonderful ability to dig in and stay put when others are taking flight at the mention of adversity or some future gain: You can bank on him/her to be there through thick and thin.	Wonderful ability to be excited by a sense of anticipation or preconception of something good ahead; amazing propensity to conjure up or latch onto a pleasurable ending: great enthusiasm and energy.
Hard to lead astray, rarely fooled by false claims, schemes, or fads. Cherish his/her feet being on the ground. Don't call him/her a sinner if slow to believe, but instead admire strength in not being swayed by consumer religion or the latest fad.	Easily fueled by romance, enjoyment of fairylike or mythic thoughts, or simply anticipation of future pleasant encounter. Cherish his/her sense for the new enterprise, the new hope, the new invention. Without this personality, the world would be a dull place!

How do we promote more respect for the other? Or even better, how do we encourage the two to appreciate—and even adopt into their own approach—the best of the other?

When There Is Conflict, Avoid the "Binocular Trick"

Cognitive therapists refer to the "binocular trick" as the distorted thinking practiced by a distraught individual who focuses *away* from his strengths. These unbalanced perceptual assessments, such as magnifying weakness and shrinking strengths, inevitably lead to negative mood states, such as depression.

Partners in marriage are prone to practicing the binocular trick *on their partner!* When we live for a period of time around a person who possesses a wonderful quality, there is an inevitable tendency to take that quality for granted. As a mate, I must keep turning the binoculars back on the *curiosa felicitas* and God-given "intelligences" of a mate that *only a marital partner can be privy to observe and fully appreciate!*

For example, my wife has an extraordinary ability to remain cheerful, even when negative circumstances befall her. I marvel at her amazing buoyancy! With incredible genius, she finds something upbeat or positive, while reeling from being stung with some event of outrageous misfortune. I am beginning to understand why "every cloud has a silver lining" in her mind: God made her an envisioner! Her imagination pencils in future possibilities that are always colored with a transcendent tint. She believes with radiant expectancy that the future will work out just fine!

GROWTH FOR AN EXAMINER

As any cognitive therapist will tell you, this envisioner *mind-set* always results in a buoyant *"mood-set."* That is, since *thoughts* precede *feelings,* the positive slant to her envisioner "future filter" inevitably produces a cheerful mood. This self-righting state of emotional equilibrium is something that a more cynical examiner like myself can only marvel at—and ponder. I wonder... *is it absorbable?* Because I understand the source of her buoyancy (her perception filter), *could I appropriate it for my life as well?* Absolutely! I can chose to put any thought into my mind that I deem helpful and healthy. Thanks to Helen's example, as an acknowledged examiner, I now have the opportunity to monitor and alter my automatic thinking patterns with greater precision and insight.

A buoyant thought always results in a buoyant feeling.

I listen carefully to the way she reacts to a negative situation, first grasping the possible consequences, then instinctively searching for some positive aspect. Even if the situation is a "no" or "rejection," she goes on with a line of thinking that *believes* "every closed door means the opening of some future door."

The more I appreciate Helen's genius, the more intrigued I become with incorporating it into my own filter! Understanding that my narrow examiner mind-set could use this new tool, I make myself ask, "How would Helen respond to this?" Since adding this new color to my perception filter, I find my spirit better fortified to fight off my old enemy of cynicism. It is a beleaguered examiner's constant enemy of the spirit! Life is sunnier!

Of course, over time I am tempted to take Helen's ability for granted, but I have resolved to find ways to keep turning the "binoculars" back on such strengths. Therapists use the phrase, "Catch her being good." (Most unhappy mates are *exceptionally skilled* at "catching their mate being bad"!) Because she is an envisioner and I am an examiner, the curious genius of Helen's qualities is often 180 degrees different from mine, as outlined below. As I look at envisioner proficiencies, I appreciate more profoundly than ever the wonders of her capacity to see things that I wouldn't. She is clearly a well-endowed envisioner—so skillful at the visionary perceptions of a situation in all of its radiant possibilities, improbabilities, opportunities, and potentialities. She's just plain *good* at it!

How good are you at "catching him/her being good"?

She is so good at it that it forces a decision of integrity upon me: either I must acknowledge this goodness, or something in my spirit dies. The real question then becomes for me, a fact-based guy, how attuned am I to "catching her being good," seeing her God-bestowed qualities—and incorporating some of *her* approach into *my* life? For as my discernment skill grows in more deeply *appreciating* each beautiful gift of God, so do I grow as well!

As skill in appreciation of another expands, so, in like manner, does your appreciation of life expand.

You can use the chart below at any time to maintain your "binoculars" on your mate's perceptual proficiencies. Use it to "catch him/her being good." Do it for your mate's sake—and I guarantee that *you* will grow as well!

Perceptual Proficiencies or "Intelligences"

Examiner	Envisioner
observant, fact-based comprehension; adroit awareness of present realities and situational limitations	imaginative, change-based comprehension; adroit awareness of present opportunities and situational possibilities

draws on past experiences to capably solve problems or see flaws in advance: rarely makes factual errors	draws on vision of imaginative possibilities to initiate change or energize others through enthusiasm for the future: likes to originate big or exciting new projects or actions
traditional leaders who respect hierarchy and convention, and monitor process carefully; adept at discerning or critiquing the factual core of a situation—good at precise work	innovative leaders who are imaginative and comfortable with start-up operations; conceptualize, design, and implement forcefully when they have a new goal or vision—good at understanding the big picture or the whole system.
preferred work/relational environment: structured, stable, predictable	preferred work/relational environment: creative, fresh, variety

Rod confessed that in his opinion, Hillary was often overly optimistic. "If she fell off of a ten-story building," he declared, "nine floors down she would be saying, 'So far, so good'"!

On the other hand, Hillary admitted that, like other envisioners, she often gets a kick out of strictly conventional, stuffy examiner types. Like the pretense-bound, know-it-all physician who wrote in his medical notes, "On the second day the knee was better, and on the third day it disappeared." When we laugh at our particular personality foibles, we demolish the enemy of pretense and denial, and get to the core of our *real* personality!

Self-depreciation, as well as honest affirmation, can be an integral part of your admiration of the innate "proficiencies" listed below. Have you focused lately on any of the following cherishing factors in your opposite?

Potential Cherishing Factors
(Circle those that apply to your mate.)

Examiner	*Envisioner*
pragmatic, easygoing: *safe to be with*	enthusiastic, cheerful: *fun to be with*
reliable, realistic: *helpful to be with*	playful, tolerant: *relaxing to be with*
sensible, analytical: *interesting to be with*	spontaneous, pleasant: *never boring to be with*
brings trustworthiness to relationship: *secure to be with*	brings vitality to relationship: *enlivening to be with*

A Common Examiner/Envisioner Clash: Religion

With their differing personalities, Rod and Hillary had clashing approaches to religion. This caused conflict every Sunday morning. Hillary was very committed to her church and spiritual values. On the other hand, Rod was a hesitant seeker of God, placing more trust in science and the observable universe. Every Sunday, Hillary believed it was important to take her children to church, whereas Rod wanted to have the freedom to go places on their day off.

WORKING WITH THE BIAS OF DIFFERING PERCEPTION FILTERS

What is the most persuasive way to relate to a person with an opposite perception filter? Let's take Rod and Hillary as our example. After I showed them the characteristics of their respective types, I encouraged them to implement a slightly different approach to the other. And things began to change!

For example, it became much easier for Hillary to relate to Rod when she began to understand why it was more palatable for him to find God through concrete or tangible evidence, such as in nature. Because he was an examiner, he was open to the grandeur of nature as something he could *touch, see, and sensually enjoy!* When they went to the mountains, he was far more open to discussing the mysteries of spirituality and God with Hillary from this common starting place. Hillary filed this away in her mind: for Rod, the observable universe was a comfortable (tangible, factual) starting place for further exploration of God's existence.

Rod's view of Hillary changed as well. He came to see her as an envisioner who tends to see the world through the gyroscope of her inner experience. It was easier for Hillary than for Rod to cast a spiritual perspective upon some common event. She shared much in common with Brother Lawrence, the seventeenth-century monk known for sensing the presence of God even amid the pots and pans of the monastery kitchen. He could speak of "feeling extremely known of God today and caressed by Him." Because of her keen attunement and affinity with the inner world of intuitive experience, Hillary easily identified with personalities like Lawrence and other spiritual leaders. Their transcendent, mysterious experiences—whether objectively verified or not—were comfortably compatible with her belief "filter."

Rather than seeing this as a naïveté or intellectual weakness, Rod came to appreciate the nourishment that Hillary gleaned from being so open to the realm of awe, wonder, and potentiality. This new appreciation for her approach had its inevitable effect, as shown below.

Growth for an Examiner: The Challenge of the Unseen Future

As Rod and Hillary sat in church one Sunday, something interesting happened to Rod. The pastor was observing the hopeless spirit of the disciples as they reacted to the sight of a foggy figure walking on the water, crying, "It's a ghost!" Their focus was trapped in a sensory fixation upon the immediate scene, blocking vision of potential other options. It was a clear-cut examiner characteristic, Rod noted.

But such was not the case for Peter, a prime example of the envisioner type. He had the audacity to call out to the shadowy figure, "Lord, if it is you, bid me come to you on the water!" The pastor asked the congregation, "Do you tend to trust too much in the tried and true? Could there be a Godly call to you right now to embrace a vision that requires moving out of your preferred, comfortable way of thinking about things?"

Rod had been silently pondering leaving his safe position with an aerospace company. It meant facing the unknown adventure of working for himself as a sole proprietor. He realized it was his "moment of truth." Could he believe in, and act upon, his gut feeling—his unscientific, immeasurable inner vision of wonderful success in his own business? This urging was propelled by the sheer excitement of a possibility that held no certain guarantee of success.

Rod began to reframe his thoughts, saying to himself, "Hillary is right on this point." My thinking sometimes "conforms me to the world" of the seen and status quo. I wish I possessed more of her proficiency in this dimension of looking into the unseen future! (Note: As soon as you begin to genuinely appreciate an intelligence other than your own, you are on the road to having some of it yourself!) Rod was starting to grow!

Growth for an Envisioner

Because envisioners like Hillary depend so much on the fuel of their visions, they are vulnerable to two major perceptual flaws. The first is the lure of a foolish vision, and sometimes brushing aside valid questions about its viability. Once they grab onto a vision, envisioners are going to run with it! This is where Hillary needed to incorporate the scrutinized insight provided by Rod's more critical, discerning filter. His lens naturally checks the data coming through, looking for what is solid or sham, truth or fiction. His natural bent is to consider everything dubious that has not been proven. If you are an envisioner, your examiner can offer insightful information you may have minimized or brushed aside.

The other temptation can strike when the envisioner's dream crashes. The "death of a dream is a sad thing," and no one knows it better than an envisioner! What happens when the slowly dying dream is that of achieving *satisfaction within her marriage?* Envisioners are extremely prone to fall into the lure of a sullen melancholia, often projected unfairly toward their mates. As Hugo put it, there is a perverse "pleasure in being sad." Envisioners who have lost hope for a happy marriage can grow wistful and paralyzed by their depressive line of thinking. If they are relater types (see chapter 1) with dependent tendencies, they can too easily attribute the source of their "slough of depression" directly to the actions of their spouse.

This marital disease is called the "projection trick" or the "attribution error." It is simply the misplacement of responsibility for our own feelings upon our mate. Actually, it is our *own thoughts* that create our *own feelings.* As a cognitive therapist, I pointed out to Hillary that while our mate's *behavior* may be disappointing, it is the nature of our thoughts *about that* behavior that actually create our sad feelings.

How do you end a paralysis of mood? The paralysis ends, like "magic," when you find an alternative line of thinking, moving from the "old view" to a "new view." For example, as a hospice counselor in earlier years, I would often note the unusual strength that some people would bring to hearing the physician's news of their imminent death. These "super-strong" individuals more often than not applied the same thought-processing method to facing death that they had brought to facing life: they would not allow themselves to give in to "misery thinking" for any length of time! While momentarily knocked down, they went about the task of finding within their difficulty some means of personal growth or positive movement toward "a better state."

Unhappy, vulnerable envisioners may need to do a fearless thought-analysis inventory. It starts by asking the painfully hard question: "Am I guilty of the 'projection trick'?"

ENVISIONERS AND EMOTIONAL REASONING

If an envisioner is also a relater type, she may fall into "emotional reasoning." Here is the assumption: If you feel it very *strongly,* it must reflect *reality.* For example, Hillary was saying to herself, "I will never achieve my dream of marital happiness living with him. I just know it. I can feel it strongly, intuitively. It must be true." But this line of reasoning will trigger predictable results: self-pity, hypochondria, or hopelessness. (Another woman, with a different filter, might see—and therefore experience—the situation quite differently.) Emotional reasoning can lead to a paralysis of mood. Note the following examples of healthy and unhealthy marital reasoning:

Healthy thinking:	"Every problem has within it the seeds of opportunity, including a marriage to an opposite personality type."
Distorted thinking:	(Emotional reasoning) "I cannot be happy married to him/her because I feel so discouraged...that I don't see how the relationship can ever get any better." Or, "the whole basis of our feelings for one another has changed."

Hillary learned to *challenge* her emotional reasoning with the hard evidence of Rod's personality traits: were they truly as unrewarding as her negative filter was portraying them? She saw that she needed to find a new vision, a new dream to hang her hat on. If you are an envisioner and your perceived loss is particularly tied to some of the limitations of being married to an examiner type, note carefully his or her strengths in this chapter. Then ask if some new visions of happiness can be found within the confines of his/her consistent, conventional ways.

Practice the powerful Splinter Principle (chapter 1) of placing your focus not on what's wrong with your partner (the splinter), but on the self-development areas in which you need to grow (your log). Answer the following assessment about where you tend to focus your cognitive energy:

Questions for a "Fearless Mental Moral" Inventory

1. Ask yourself, is *too much* of my happiness dependent on my mate behaving a certain way? (Is your happiness dependent upon your mate's conforming to *your vision* of a particular marital model, or dream that you cling to from the past?)
2. Does your idealistic inner model say to you, *"This is the* not *the way I conceived how our happy marriage* should *look?* (Some people live in misery under a pile of self-constructed "shoulds"! Carefully examine

your own pile of "shoulds" as possible perfectionist expectations of your mate or the marriage itself. Get out from under the pile now!)

3. Could it be that you were destined to grow more whole and complete by virtue of being married to a more cautious type who challenges the way you believe the world "should" work?

4. Is it possible for you to slightly alter your vision rather than waiting for him to change his conventional ways—which may take years, or never happen? (Remember the Splinter Principle.)

5. Are there some opportunities for personal growth in terms of learning to stay put and turning your mountainous problem into a gold mine of transcendent growth?

STRESS AND BELIEF SYSTEMS: THE OPTIMISTIC EXPLANATORY STYLE

Studies have proven that persons with an internal locus of control handle marital and personal stress better. These people believe that to a great extent they control their own destinies. Others possess an external locus of control, believing that chance or outside forces determine their fate. In study after study, internals achieve more in school, feel less depressed than do externals, and cope better with various stresses, including marital problems. Psychologist Martin Seligman, in studying stress resilience, defined this characteristic of hardy types as an "optimistic explanatory style." When a negative event occurred, these types "attributed it" or *believed* it to be an isolated and temporary occurrence rather than part of a general trend or persistent pattern of life. In *Learned Optimism* (Knopf, New York, 1998), Seligman explains how you can gain a brighter outlook on life by changing your thinking habits responsible for your "explanatory style." This centers in the way you explain setbacks to yourself.

I am reminded of a story about S. I. Hayakawa, who was looking out of his hotel window one day upon the scene of busy Indiana Street below. It is a street often blocked by badly parked cars and huge trailer trucks whose maneuvering often caused frustrating traffic jams. Adding to the chaos was the streetcar line going down the middle of the street.

He watched as some of the motormen who were blocked would get steamed up, clang their bells with rage, and shout at the drivers. At the end of the day, they were undoubtedly nervous wrecks or drained shells.

Other motormen, he noted, could sit and patiently wait for minutes at a time. They would calmly whistle a tune, or clean their equipment or nails without a trace of excessive agitation. It was as if they were saying, "What a great job I have!"

I quoted the research literature with Rod, noting that certain areas of belief, such as the unforeseen future, require going beyond an examiner's natural bent for evidence. When it comes to questions beyond the observable, science cannot explain "why." For example, *why* do these "optimistic types," who make leaps of faith and live their lives with "positive visions," do better? While the science of psychology cannot explain *why* they do, it can document that this is a *fact*.

I reflected back to Rod the agnostic, "As you stated, you can see the benefit to Hillary of her faith. Belief in God empowers her to view the future as an undeniably exciting, positive concept. It is colored this way by her perception filter, her belief that examiners have to admit that, when circumstances *appear* intractable to us, the envisioner approach is broader, freeing, and happier."

"It is the happier way, without a doubt," Rod agreed.

"Psychology cannot impart an optimistic belief system into the mind and soul of a person," I continued. "Are you open to incorporating some more of her type of positive future perceptions into your thinking patterns? Are you willing to add a little room for the 'unseen' good that may come along, for 'surprising new serendipities' as you form your schema of the future?"

BELIEFS AND CHANGING THE MOOD OF A MARRIAGE

Unhappy couples come to therapists wanting to know how to change the mood of their marriage. Over a period of time, we all fall into thought patterns that precipitate certain mood states. If a couple is stuck in a recurring negative pattern of beliefs toward one another, how can they alter their established pattern? One technique is to point out the ability to separate the interpretation (based on beliefs) of events from the events themselves. That is, events in the world have no inherent meaning: meaning is created in our minds by the *beliefs* we assign to them.

In marriage, a mate's behavior has no inherent meaning in and of itself. Meaning comes only when you interpret the behavior in your mind, believing it to be positive or negative. Once we realize that *we* are the ones who assign it validity and thereby give it power, it dawns on us that we also have the option of changing our belief and thereby gaining control over its ability to effect us. We do this by challenging our thoughts with the question, "Is this the only possible interpretation (*the* truth), or is it one of several alternative possible interpretations (*a* truth)?" Could your interpretation be based upon half-blinded perspective? If it is one of several possible perspectives, now you begin to decrease its hold on your mind and mood.

The next time you think a negative thought about your mate, see if you can then conceive of a second or alternative thought that renders your mate in a better light. This should be an "opposite side of the coin" or "shed in a different light" thought. Even if you remain quite convinced that your first thought is the most accurate, if the second has a more pleasant effect on your mood, why not live in that state for a while? When you make this choice, you separate yourself from the "victimization" feeling of having to live solely in the miserable shadow of another's "strange" personality.

PRACTICAL PRINCIPLES FOR EXAMINERS AND ENVISIONERS

Remember to practice the power of empathy found in the Kenosis Principle, trying to enter more deeply into your opposite's frame of reference in order to understand and appreciate it as though it were your own perspective. It is an act of the will that *never fails to communicate love.*

One of the great monarchs in Persia was known as a champion of the common people. To relate to their needs and problems, he would mingle with them in various disguises. He once befriended a poor man who tended a furnace at the public baths, and over the course of time they became good friends, talking about each other's loneliness and sharing plain food together. The poor man grew to love him deeply.

Then one day, the shah revealed his true identity and position. Expecting to hear a request for some expensive gift, the shah was surprised when his subject sat silently gazing at him in awe. Finally, he said respectfully, "You left your palace and ease to sit with me, eat my coarse bread, and care whether my heart is glad or sad. Please, your majesty, while you give rich presents to others, you have given yourself to me—never withdraw the priceless gift of your friendship."

Empathy is an act that conveys caring, even if one shares a different "status" or belief system! Empathy does not mean that you agree with another's beliefs, only that you seek to emotionally and intellectually understand them.

Consider the following as practical ways to practice empathy with your opposite in the realm of differing beliefs:

How an Examiner Can Better Relate to an Envisioner

Emotional/Spiritual Principle 1	Energy is generated by a belief system with a hope-filled sense of the future.
Personality Principle 1	*Be sensitive to the energizing vision of your envisioner (you could use some of this energy).*

Envisioners want inspiration that fits into their vision or model of the world, which will nourish them and fuel their passion for life! Make sure you "see" and understand the current vision of your envisioner—particularly his vision of a "happy marriage." Get him to express his vision or model in explicit terminology, which may be difficult. (I often make them write out their explicit dreams—it's hard work for envisioners, but worth it!) Envisioners generally don't focus a lot on details in the present scene, viewing the present as something that is temporary, elusive, and often irrelevant. They place their stock only in the current paradigm that is lighting their fire.

So, your task is to find a juicy ingredient of your envisioner's model that is positively enticing to you as well. Find an element of the inspiration that is pure or lovely, excellent or glorious, exciting or magnificent to you. If you can't find anything, you are: (1) not trying hard enough, or (2) repressing your own dreams, which is not uncommon for extreme examiners, who can easily fall prey to the enemy of cynicism!

Then verbally express your agreement and affirmation. As an advocate and partner, make some promises and plans to help make this aspect of her/his vision a reality. Let the passion from the vision flow!

For example, planting flowers as an examiner, I have a tendency to think of all the things that could possibly go wrong. I try to anticipate these things, and even tend to guardedly prepare myself for the fact that they may die and I will fail. On the other hand, my envisioner mate, Helen, will assume that they will probably take root, and are likely to grow in a healthy manner, given proper conditions. She tends to assume the best, and I tend to assume the worst! Is this any way to run a garden? Absolutely!

Without a juicy vision of some beautiful flowering plants, I would probably not try to plant anything at all! Her enthusiastic vision for adding some vibrant color to the front porch pushes me over the indecisive edge of my doubts, making it worth a try. She states that she doesn't care if they die, and realizes that they might. But her emphasis is on the trying, the vision, and the possibility.

This partnership of her energizing, venturesome envisioner spirit coupled with my cautious, prudent examiner spirit makes the endeavor of planting—and life itself—fun!

I'm slowly learning: *Be sensitive to the energizing vision of your envisioner. Among other benefits, you could use some of this energy yourself!*

Emotional/Spiritual Principle 2	When each partner deems himself or herself as half blind regarding the future, full vision becomes possible only through incorporation of the perceptions of both.
Personality Principle 2	*Find common threads when beliefs conflict.*

When you present facts contrary to an envisioner's vision, be ready to meet great resistance. You may feel minimized or ignored, so look hard for common threads when the *present data* (which you value and want to present) appears to contradict your mate's futuristic vision. Affirm that the vision is exciting and that, at some genuine and albeit smaller degree, you share it as well.

Envisioners tend to imaginatively see alternatives and opportunities but often overlook the present factual scene. If you are going to present facts that could be seen as oppositional, make sure that they are perceived as relevant and necessary to *balance and ground the vision*—but not to attack or destroy it. Never destroy enthusiasm: go with it—by making the effort to *find common threads when beliefs and approaches are in conflict.*

Emotional/Spiritual Principle 3	To have a soul-mate relationship, each person must be an autonomous, independent soul.
Personality Principle 3	*Value the courage of the independent spirit.*

In order to be a soul mate, first you must be a soul. A whole person has an independent spirit that is able to follow one's heart without fear of violating conventions or clinging dependence upon others or physical surroundings. Often, a strong envisioner will bring such strength of personality and spirit. A wise examiner will value such courage of spirit and emulate it to become a robust, complete person! The possibility of a "soul-mating journey" starts when both parties *value the courage of the independent spirit.*

In summary, you need to appreciate and emulate your envisioner's capacity for:

1. *Positive enthusiasm:* Build upon and incorporate your mate's fire, energy, and passion by catching his/her way of energizing.
2. *Optimistic collaboration:* Find common threads when beliefs conflict, and be true partners that make each others dreams come true.
3. *Courageous independence:* Autonomy is required in order for mates to be flourishing souls who can freely express themselves and their gifts.

Drawing Closer to an Examiner

Emotional/Spiritual Principle 1	Healthy beliefs are grounded in a view of reality that starts first with the current factual situation.
Personality Principle 1	*Try to be fact-based when beliefs differ.*

Examiners prefer the proof of established past patterns or traditions. If you have an idea that you want to sell, use past experience that appeals to his/her sense of truth as grounded in present or previous experience. First ask yourself, "How is the problem best defined by current facts, that is, the current situation?" Speak as if this is your starting place, and this approach will score big points with an examiner.

Note: When envisioners are married to alcoholics, they often fall into *enabling* the alcoholic by easily believing his/her recurring promises to quit drinking. This is the vision that the envisioner wants to see and wants so much to believe. Yet, what is needed is an action-based orientation. Assertively state that the *present situation,* that is, the disease of alcoholism, *must* be addressed now through immediate, specific *actions.* I suggest immediate involvement in a 12-step program and professional therapy (including marriage therapy).

Emotional/Spiritual Principle 2	An imaginative vision or possibility may be realistic or a passing illusion or fantasy. Get feedback or corroboration from others *before* you proceed.

Personality Principle 2   *Show corroboration when presenting ideas—if possible.*

The most persuasive perceptions for an examiner will be those that can be verified, that is, measured, tracked, and corroborated by some history. Examiners prefer the evidence of direct, concrete facts. Hence, ask yourself, "What have others said about this issue? Would they corroborate my view?" In your discussions with an examiner, note both those who oppose your vision as well as those who agree with it. Relate *first* that you see the scene as it really is, or how others see it; and *then* note how *you* see it or would like it to be.

Every futuristic dream must, like a climb up Mt. Everest, start with a trek in the foothills where acclimation takes place. Such yearnings can become accustomed to reality by patiently dealing with the challenges of the realistic, well-grounded examiner. Anticipate the examiner's grounding questions, and *show the corroboration of others whenever you can.*

Personality Principle 3   *Keep the binoculars on your mate's proficiencies, not limitations.*

Examiners are often slow, cautious, and pragmatic souls whom envisioners can easily label boring and dull. Taking the consistent, steady approach to life, they typically focus on present responsibilities. Consequently, they may be quite trustworthy, majoring in such things as showing love by being a steadfast breadwinner. If they are spiritually minded, they are often uncommonly faithful, consistent, and reliable.

Therefore, they deserve appreciation from an envisioner who could tend to overlook the benefits that are enjoyed due to such plodding, day-to-day efforts. If you open your belief filter to include appreciation of his/her focus upon the guaranteed and certain, you can gain a more profound, heartfelt sense of appreciation of your current blessings and status. Such benefits can be easily overlooked or taken for granted by the more global, passionate belief orientation of a typical envisioner. *Keep the binoculars on your mate's proficiencies, not limitations.*

In summary, work at incorporating and appreciating the examiner's capacity for:

1. *Powerful observation:* Use it to establish your beliefs and make them better grounded in reality!
2. *Thorough investigation:* It makes examiner belief systems sensible, realistic, and worth listening to before you embark!

3. Keep your binoculars focused on your mate's proficiencies—and your appreciation of current blessings and advantages will grow!

INTEGRATING BELIEF SYSTEMS

When the belief systems of examiners and envisioners collide, there is great potential for frustration—or enhancement—of the effectiveness of both. Enhancement comes through integrating the best of both "filters," converting them into a common approach to the world represented in *both present situational facts and future possibilities*. Examiners and envisioners need each other. Such integration cannot help but refine the wisdom of your beliefs, making them deeper, wider, and more satisfying.

SPIRITUALITY PROFILES OF AN EXAMINER AND ENVISIONER

The Examiner as a Spiritual Type

Examiners will tend to seek God as found in the immediate and concrete. Their preference for data in the present scene or status quo will lead them to trust in the tried-and-true institutions of church or religion. They will look toward pragmatic and literal forms of religious experience, having to "see" miracles before they believe them! More reliable and comfortable spirituality is found in a physical universe that they can see, touch, and verify. Open their senses to smell the pines or salt air, or view a crystal blue sky behind a mountain lake, and they have found heaven-on-Earth!

In terms of regular spiritual practice, they tend to find spiritual satisfaction or God's will in faithful obedience to some obvious human need. For example, an obvious current community problem or local cause might draw their interest. They will be slow to warm to what they would consider a "grandiose" mission or far-fetched crusade schema.

The "cross of discomfort" they tend to avoid is the hazy vagueness of an exciting vision or imaginative future opportunity. Whereas Peter looks out of the boat in a storm and sees the vision of Jesus walking on the water, the examiner type looks out and cries, "It's a ghost!" They can easily fall into a doubtful thinking pattern that causes them to stay in stale, outdated paradigms and create fearful rationalizations. The paralysis of analysis can deter them from venturing forth into their occasional exciting dreams or visions. They need to develop a growing consciousness and sensitivity that God is communicating to them through such ideas.

In general, for spiritual completeness, the examiner needs to develop greater capacity to embrace hopeful anticipation and imagination. He needs to expand his capacity for heightened awareness of realms beyond his immediate focus and emotional attachment, letting go of fear of change and venturing more often into the unknown.

The Envisioner as a Spiritual Type

Envisioners look for God in the form of an exciting future vision, schema, or possibility beyond the current scene. With their keen propensity for anticipation and/or an inner assurance born of the inspiration of their vision, they often see signs or indications that God is near or at work. These signs, often esoteric, comprise a kind of prophetic foretelling of good things to come. Heaven-on-Earth is found in these occasional subjective, aesthetic, or mystical experiences of union with God.

The "cross of discomfort" for envisioners is having their vision challenged as impractical, or having it crash. Sometimes they will stubbornly stick to their vision, ignoring facts, and going beyond a reasonable time to give up and move on. They may close their mind to the grounding message needed to adjust their dream as it confronts limitation. Limitations can also be an expression of God's will.

For example, Jesus experienced just such limitation. He prayed for his own vision ("that this cup pass from me"), yet he also prayed for direction to find harmony with the Father's plan ("Your will be done"). These limitations may be the guideposts of God asking them to remain faithful within a current, confining boundary. Such boundaries can prod development of "patience with joy" or endurance.

For example, their cross may mean involvement in the present focus of some service or ministry that grounds them in the grit of human limitation. Or, it may mean appropriating the feedback of "fact-based" reality as offered by their examiner partner into the paradigm that drives them— without losing the enthusiasm for its exciting promise.

In general, in order to be spiritually complete, envisioners need to be grounded through some reality-based embodiment of their vision.

CONCLUSION

The role of your mate's perception "filter" is key to understanding how to approach him or her when beliefs differ. If you don't think perception is important, consider the story of the elderly couple resting after the celebration of their seventy-fifth wedding anniversary. Sitting silently on the porch in their rocking chairs, the wife was the first to speak. "John, I'm proud of you."

"Would you speak up, Mildred?" he loudly replied. "You know I'm hard of hearing!"

In a louder voice, she replied, "John, I'm proud of you!"

"I can't hear you, Mildred!" he replied. "Would you speak up?"

"John, I'm proud of you!" she practically yelled in his ear.

"Oh ... well, yes. I'm tired of you, too," he replied!

Perception filters can really distort our views of reality! Make sure you know—and appreciate—your mate's approach to belief systems.

Chapter 6

SEX WITH AN OPPOSITE: MAKING IT GOOD FOR BOTH

Sex begins at dinner.

This statement captures the pivotal role of emotional connection in a couple's sex life. When each feels close to the other, sexual desire follows as naturally as spring follows winter. The Creator intended that couples mutually revel in the joy of lovemaking, including the pleasures of natural sensuality and libido (see *The Song of Solomon,* The Holy Bible). So, sex should be as easy as "falling off a wagon," right?

Wrong! Just as we have seen in the other personality areas, the clash of differing personalities can distort things—including the chemistry of sexual attraction. We instinctively want to have our approach validated. This is even more poignantly true in sexuality, an area so close to the center of our identity that it often raises core issues of acceptability and vulnerability. In therapy, I watch usually talkative couples become like stuttering mutes when conversation turns to this area of tender egos, specific personal preferences, and, all too often, agonizing disappointment. Without understanding, sexual frustration stemming from a personality difference leads to a pitched battle rather than the pleasurable "dessert after the main course" that it's designed to be.

THE FORMATION OF SEXUAL CHEMISTRY

Sexual attraction is much more than mere physical attraction.

Webster correctly defines "eros" or erotic pleasure as the *aggregate of sexual pleasure instincts*. It is an inclusive, "wanting-to-be-with" attraction to the opposite gender felt by both sexes. While they have basically the same need—to be together (the urge to merge)—they often feel that pull differently. I want to suggest how the *pull of eros* may be influenced by the *particular personality approach* of each mate.

On the following pages, I have identified eight forms of eros as potentially shaped by personality. Identification of each mate's particular way of expressing this drive can hopefully be a helpful guide because intimacy is fostered by awareness. The goal is to dispel *some* of the mystery of each mate's sexual inclinations (it's a deep and complex mystery!), and create greater understanding. Remember, sex begins at dinner because *closeness plays the pivotal role* in a satisfying sex life.

NEEDED FOR GROWTH WITH AN OPPOSITE PERSONALITY

Reasoner: emotive eros
or
Relater: sensory eros

Examiner: romantic eros
or
Envisioner: cherishing eros

Reflector: empathetic eros
or
Activator: attending eros

Planner: emancipating eros
or
Journeyer: reasoning eros

Since you and I feel the drive of eros through our personality filter, we must start with the most important sexual organ of them all.

The Most Important Sexual Organ: The Brain

The brain is where our attitudes and feelings toward our mate are formed. Sexual chemistry follows each personality's preferred pathway, which is an often subconscious pattern of automatic thinking. Whether we are aware of this process or not, these pathways steer us toward particular qualities in another person. If you identify your personality preference pathways in sexuality, you'll better understand why you are attracted to some people and behaviors, and repulsed by others.

"I have a crush on him."

"Why are you attracted to him?" comes the response of a puzzled friend who possesses a personality preference quite different from yours.

The following categories of automatic thinking define, in general categories, the peculiar hidden drives that wire you toward certain characteristics of another—that is, which personality characteristics "turn you on" and "turn you off." These categories are offered because:

1. *Sexual preferences are sometimes hard to talk about.* Use these "profiles" as a conversation starter in your relationship. While some want quick, black-and-white answers about sex, sexuality is a mystery too profound for "precise categorical solutions." So expect to identify with some of my suggested traits and not with others.

2. *Categories can suggest starting places.* Stereotyping can be helpful, but should not be taken too literally. While I employ the same "titles" of personality preferences from previous chapters, *do not* assume a direct one-to-one correlation between personality type and sexuality type.

As you read, find yourself first, and then find your mate. (I know you probably can't resist "typing" him or her!) Then earmark the areas where you can develop in the promising world of understanding different approaches to sex.

THE DIFFERING APPROACHES TO SEXUALITY

The Reasoner and the Relater

Reasoner	Relater
automatic thinking in decision-making approach to sexual activity	automatic thinking in decision-making approach to sexual activity
(most often males, but not always)	(most often females, but not always)
In the head—formal	In the heart—sentimental
Can be detached from body urges (libido) by disruptive thinking patterns (e.g., performance anxiety, stress). These issues can become a rationale to avoid initiation of sexual activity.	Can be detached from body urges (libido) by disruptive relationship events (e.g., fight, critical words). These feelings can become a rationale to avoid responding to the initiation of sexual activity.

Greatest Fears and Inhibitions:

Reasoner	Relater
Revealing raw emotions that he works hard to conceal: usually fear of failure or impotence. Most relaters do not understand the depth of this fear and minimize it.	Revealing on the stage of sexual encounter parts of herself well hidden: usually fear of loneliness or rejection. Most reasoners do not understand the depth of this fear and minimize it.

Physical refusal can be taken as if person is somehow defective: *"I'm not acceptable or desirable."* His masculine ego may be threatened as if he is "odd," incompetent, or lacking the masculine strength to get his needs met.

Emotional distraction can be taken personally: *"He just wants sex"* (often to unload his suppressed feelings and relax). She may feel "used" and distant from him if taken personally, feeling a lack of consideration for her needs.

Physical rejection can suggest to him that he may never find the potentially frequent, ecstatic, pleasuring gratification initially conceived when she entered into marriage. It is the death of his dream: his dearest sexual hopes and fantasies may never be consummated.

Emotional rejection can suggest to her that she may never find the potentially comforting, warm, secure gratification she expected when she entered into marriage. It is the death of her dream: her dearest sentiments about relational intimacy, security, and comfort may never be enjoyed.

When he succumbs to the personalization error (chapter 1), he may blame his mate and then turn to other sexual outlets to reduce his suppressed angst, such as pornography, another woman, or other sources of gratification.

When she succumbs to the personalization error (chapter 1), she may blame her mate and turn a cold shoulder to him sexually to convey her distress. She may then turn her focus to children, homemaking, or to other sources of gratification.

Developmental Opportunities for the Reasoner and Relater

The Reasoner: Emotional Eros

Exploring the shadowy side of his sexuality approach can be the means of profound development for the reasoner!

If you are a typical reasoner, you are unfamiliar with, and fearful of, deep feelings. Like the dark floor of the ocean bottom, the deep feelings of intense passion and commitment to another are particularly foreign to your experience. You can, however, tap into these latent feelings if you will give yourself permission to move into uncharted waters. You can find yourself drawn into wondrous new realms of discovery about intimate bonding with your mate.

Not the least of these discoveries is an awakening passion for all of life! This comes because an energizing force is often buried deep within the emotionally starved reasoner. It lies untapped until the intensity of the sexual encounter sparks its ignition! By temporarily setting aside your preferred "in-the-head" approach, you can find yourself catapulted onto a magic carpet ride...to the scary but adventuresome land of unexplored, unexpressed, passionate feeling!

For example, I find myself occasionally saying to my wife during sex, "I never knew I could love someone so much!" Feelings of warm energy and a pulsing, fiery vibrancy flood my being. As this flame of passion ignites my soul, I sometimes feel as if I have found a new part of myself. It is like a dark corner in the basement of my emotions that has been lying in the shadows all these years. Each time I travel to this new place, I feel as excited as a young lad on Christmas morning. What a wonderful ride to new heights and depths of sheer ecstasy (who needs the drug!).

Fellow reasoners, these sexual highs are just the tip of the iceberg as we begin to uncover the treasures of deeper emotional experience! These treasures beckon to the courageous reasoner who is willing to open his personality to the discovery of new dimensions of himself. Grasp the doorknob, open the door, and cross the threshold into the beckoning realm of *emotional eros!*

How does a reasoner do this? First, he must recognize that when he "stays in his head," his intellect becomes a barrier to full experience of deeper feelings. The defensive armor worn by many a gallant knight in battle blocks out the natural expression of direct, primal feeling. For many reasoners, this feeling level lays out of reach, awaiting the oxygen of discovery through sexuality. Before sex, the knight needs to undress both *physically and emotionally.* For example, he may state that confusing feelings of being both a brave knight and a scared little boy live simultaneously within him. On any given night, he may allow the playful, spontaneous little boy within him to run loose. Or he may permit the needy, dependent child within him to express his desire for comfort or support. Whenever he is in any of these states and he makes a complete, direct connection with his feelings (not his intellect), he is moving toward the wholeness of *emotional eros.*

In the state of *emotional eros,* the reasoner can feel accepted when his shadow side yearns to be sheltered or comforted by an understanding female. (She should do this in a soft, understanding, companionship mode—and not in a mothering mode, which makes him feel dependent.) While his instinctual desire is affirmation of his ego, which is often his status or success as a man, he must learn to turn his "am I performing well" mind off (finally!). Here he can find the relaxation that he deeply needs in the afterglow of verbal intercourse that flows when beautiful emotions are unleashed. This is the manhood of deepening emotional awareness and dialogue—the wondrous, beckoning realm of *emotional eros.*

A genuinely masculine "stallion" (as a reasoner would prefer!) is able to reveal his anxiety, anger, and disappointment. A stallion can freely emote, sharing his heart as well as his concerns, not only about his knightly work-day battles, but also about his experience of life in general. Rather than appearing distracted to his sensitive mate prior to having sex, he elimi-nates much, if not all, of the mystery of his apparent distance. (Reasoners stuck in their intellect are often accurately sensed as preoccupied or "else-where" by relationally proficient relaters.)

Reasoners need to keep in mind that the sensitive mate may sense his distraction and feel used, as if she is some sort of emotional outlet, a dumping ground for getting rid of his workday anxiety or angst. She needs to understand that when this happens, many of his repressed feel-ings are actually manifesting themselves—and she should not take it per-sonally, which is difficult for relaters. These feelings should be ventilated at dinner or during a quiet time by being verbalized in an assertive, healthy manner. When they aren't, the repressed need for relaxation after a stress-filled day, for example, may send off a distorted message of self-absorption to his mate. Such messages become barriers to honest bond-ing—emotionally and sexually. Whether he is conscious of it or not, what he so intensely needs and craves with his mate is the deeper experience of emotional eros.

Fellow reasoners, one possibility is to use this book as a convenient starting point. Say to your spouse, "Please listen. I need a partner. I want to move into the uncomfortable realm of exploration of my hidden self, my evolving self, and my feeling side. Can you accept me when I share some feelings that may make you uncomfortable? Can we both make a commitment to share our souls in an atmosphere of open emotional inter-course, of *emotional eros?*"

At this point, the reasoner can confront the doubts that often haunt his more intellectualized experience of life, such as success in career, self-image, marriage, or some other endeavor. Even the occasional carryover to sexuality—performance anxiety—can be swept away by honest dis-course. The intensity of sexual intercourse can sometimes propel the pro-cess by bringing deep feeling to consciousness. However, in order to fully develop this capacity, you must make a commitment to periodically risk crossing a threshold into a room where at first you feel uncomfortably vul-nerable. Still, the rule of emotional eros remains: always go *toward vul-nerability.* It is the way that real "stallions" live! It is the way Jesus lived. It is the commitment that opens the door to *emotional eros.*

Fellow reasoners, let's awake the sleeping giant within us! Remember that your relater partner can bring to you the rich gift of her proficiency in the unexplored sea of emotions from her more crystallized world of inner experience. Trust me: there is intelligence *in* these emotions yet to be plumbed by you!

Postscript: There is also a promise of spiritual growth in *emotional eros!*

The reasoner has a strong bent to strive for the comfort of a "reason-based" certitude. But in the mystery of sexuality, reasoners are often forced into embracing strange, contradicting, or chaotic conceptualizations of how sex "should be." The certitude-seeking reasoner must embrace the premise that creativity often flows from chaos, disorder, or change.

Once open to the fresh wind of chaos as a potentially positive force in life, a new interest can emerge, an intrigue in understanding the mystery—not only of sexual feelings, but other longings as well. The long dormant creativity that flows from vague or shadowy inner hungers can become more vibrant. Once you may have insisted upon reason and certitude to somehow intellectually prove that God is real. Now you can learn to be comfortable with—indeed, intrigued by—the experience of mystery. Of specific intrigue is the possibility that a mysterious, provident God is at work in inner areas of your life, including your marriage. You may well be on the cutting edge of new insights—found in the passions of *emotional eros*—or in fertile, undeveloped regions of your spirit that passionately long for serenity, love, or purpose!

For a conceptually bound reasoner, this is a fascinating prospect for self-expansion.

Developmental Opportunities for the Relater

The Development of Sensuality Eros

The relater naturally seeks the gratification of warm feelings of closeness with her mate. Yet some relaters, so focused upon this dyadic relationship, can gradually become detached from the urges of their own libido. In this case, the challenge is to develop a strong sense of your *own physical needs,* your own libido. The primal power of your innate sex drive can be experienced as quite separate from other feelings, such as the hurt from a heated argument. As a relater, you can easily develop an unhealthy dependence upon the valuation or treatment vibrations from your partner—whom you are acutely attuned to. Developing a deeper awareness of your latent sexual drive will make you a more whole person and a more attractive sex partner. I call it the wonderful joy of *sensuality eros.*

You may want to try to determine the sources of your repression, such as "old parent tapes," or a past molestation. If your repressed libido is due to Christian teaching, you should review the sensuality of Jesus in the Scriptures. He appreciated aesthetic beauty and physical sensuality, likening the loveliness of the lilies of the field to the splendid dress of Solomon in the highest days of his court. If Jesus affirmed healthy sensuality as a gift from God, then so can you!

Developing a Delight in Sensuality

How does a relater develop a deeper awareness of her natural eroticism or *sensuality eros,* as contrasted to the *emotional eros* needed by the reasoner?

The full development of a woman's erotic side can be thought of as the loss of her "erotic virginity." You can set this as your goal: the experience of complete freedom in enjoying your own body (despite any of its imperfections) and of feeling the power of sexual desire physically as well as emotionally. In my capacity as a therapist, some women have told me that they do this through complete surrender, which, at the right time, can be liberating and delicious. By any means that are appropriate for you, it is a pleasant aspect of sexuality that you are entitled to feel, even if the relational climate is less than fully harmonious.

The exciting part of this independent, autonomous approach to sex is that it adds to your happiness as a whole person. The satisfaction of being a sexually gratified woman who is in touch with her own needs builds a secure, happy self-concept. Some of your fond hopes are indeed coming true! Each erotic milestone deepens, enriches, and informs every other experience of yourself.

How can you develop your seductive side?

1. *Touch.* Most men love to be touched. Grab his arm or pat his behind.

2. *Use your eyes.* Look at him directly, with intense eye contact. Smile in a playful, energized, seductive manner that says, "I'm looking for fun, big guy. What are you going to do about it?"

3. *Kiss him.* Kiss his ear and whisper seductively into it. Push your body against his. Be comfortable enough with yourself that you can occasionally take some risks and initiate physical contact.

A brief postscript regarding sensuality eros: Your newly independent attitude toward sexual satisfaction also can bring about a spiritual benefit.

As we develop our God-given sexual nature, the fulfillment of our primal urges will spur our partner's development as well. Changes in one partner's awareness of his/her erotic (or emotional) side will inevitably alter the relationship, for we are interconnected in marriage. Finding deeper pleasures that the Grand Designer planned has a reinforcing effect. More erotic pleasure for *her* pulls *him* toward desiring greater emotional closeness to her. At the same time, more erotic pleasure for him usually results in the pleasure of greater emotional closeness for her, because intimacy begets the desire for more intimacy.

The gift of human sexuality is an incredibly amazing mechanism for bringing physical and emotional pleasure to each partner! As partners move toward wholeness, both can be grateful for the promise of more eros, more intimacy, and more miracles of personality insight to be discovered!

In summary, set about the development of sensuality eros and believe that many unimagined benefits will follow!

The Examiner and the Envisioner Approach

Consider the examiner as representative of the more physically oriented of the two partners, full of lusty enthusiasm for touching, seeing, and sensual pleasure. Trouble may be brewing if the examiner is coupled with a romantic envisioner who is keenly sensitive to the right "atmosphere." She (if the envisioner is female) is more focused on accompanying romantic amenities, such as novelty, surprise, or thoughtfulness. Here's the problem. He is an examiner, anxious to get to the real stuff, the sensory stimulation, the "examination," and the here-and-now physical experience. She is an envisioner, anxious to slow down and enjoy the best stuff, the romantic beauty, the "vision," and enlivening possibilities that comprise the rapturous atmosphere of the experience.

For a solution, let's look first at the different focus of each personality, which is often subconscious. Then we shall see how each can move toward better sexual experiences—and personal expansion—through understanding personality preferences.

Examiner	*Envisioner*
(Assumed here to be a man, but not always the case)	(Assumed here to be a woman, but not always the case)
Natural focus in sexual activity	Natural focus in sexual activity

Focus upon sensuality and intense, present state of erotic enjoyment found in touch and physical pleasuring. Great sex is defined in his (if not male, reverse these roles) mind typically in physical terms of eroticism or frequency.

Focus upon novelty and intense, anticipated state of idyllic enjoyment, romance, mutual experience of pleasure. Great sex is defined in her mind (if not female, reverse the roles) in terms of thoughtful novelty or vitality of encounter.

Lusty orientation—with desire to physically pleasure himself first, and partner second—though his enjoyment is enhanced by expression of enjoyment from physically passionate partner

Fascination orientation—with desire for new or novel experience as intriguing and most pleasurable to her—though her enjoyment is enhanced by expression of a partner who is enjoying novelty as well

Fears or Inhibitions:

Examiner

Envisioner

Afraid of changing what has worked in the past. Therefore, may settle for less or partner complains of a boring routine

Afraid of deep attachment that may feel restrictive. Therefore, may play with illusion, wishful thinking, or escapist fantasies

A Developmental Opportunity for an Examiner

The Development of Romantic Eros

If you are an examiner, expressing words of affection at the beginning of lovemaking may feel awkward. Nevertheless, you must learn to do so, even though it may feel superficial or corny at first. As the sexual intensity increases, you will find yourself pulled by the power of long ignored emotional needs. At first it may feel like you only need sex, but at deeper levels, you may find you are starved for affirmation and admiration.

When you speak adoring words, your fantasized self-concept as a man who is able to get what he wants in life finds fulfillment. You will hear in return the adoring words of your mate. This important reinforcement of your lovemaking ability happens, increasing your sense of yourself as a competent sex partner.

But in order to get to this point, you must learn to enjoy a bit of living on the cutting edge of novelty. You will need to explore new frontiers of fresh thinking and innovative ways to romance her that push you into the fear zone. There can be joy in becoming a "renaissance man" who is chivalrous because he delights in what it can do—not for him—but for his lover. Let your love for her bring out the hidden knight within you who will fearlessly stop at nothing to please his fair maiden!

This is the joy that awaits an examiner who comes to appreciate *romantic eros*.

A Developmental Opportunity for an Envisioner

The Development of Loyalty Eros

If you are an envisioner, you tend to value spontaneity and novelty. You may have a tendency to view such behavior (or lack thereof) by your mate as a gauge of how much you are valued by him/her. You may also have the tendency to lock on to a particular vision of how sex or the relationship ought to be. That vision often includes your specific preference for romance according to your particular image of idyllic rapture. (If your definition of passion is the Hollywood screen version, I suggest you bury it in favor of a more lasting one, like that "attractive, want-to-be-with-you" kind I mentioned at the beginning of the chapter).

It may be easy for you to overlook the benefits of having a regular, secure, and trustworthy sexual partner. The constancy and steadiness of your loyal partner can provide the security for a jumping off place to open up areas of awareness of your own needs. For example, while you may feel valued for the things you do, there may be a nagging insecurity or need for a deeper level of valuing at the core of your being as a *person*. You are valuable just by being yourself, without being creative, exciting, or anything else. But how can this profound discovery of your value as a *person* become forged deep into your core image of yourself?

On those days when you feel depressed or flat, your loyal partner will tell you, in word or deed, that you are still of great value to him. In fact, even sharing your depressed feelings is valuable, because they represent who you are. You are a whole person, which includes not only your upbeat outlook on life and its possibilities, but also your feelings of sadness or discouragement on down days.

Consider the fruit of loyalty. Think of some long-term married couples who, like my parents, can speak to one another with amazing frankness and candor. At times I am amazed, if not shocked, by their bluntness and total lack of pretense. This state of unabashed openness has been earned by more than a half-century of loyalty to one another. Such loyalty brings a wonderful reward: whatever difficulty arises between them, their love can handle it.

Look again at your partner's loyalty. Be thankful for the opportunity it gives you to truly be yourself. You have a consistent source of security that allows you to open up your spirit and express it—any time, any place. On a regular, daily basis, you have access to a wonderful gift—a partner you can count on. You have been granted the privilege and joy of sharing burdens with a loyal, if not chivalrous mate. You are blessed!

Don't minimize what your partner offers you with his loyal, stable ways. Learn to appreciate and enjoy all the benefits of *loyalty eros.*

The Activator and the Reflector

Activator	*Reflector*
automatic thinking: what energizes the sexual experience	automatic thinking: what energizes the sexual experience
(assumed as female for illustration purposes only)	(assumed as male for illustration purposes only)
other-centered orientation	self-centered orientation
seeks mutual experience	seeks inner-world gratification
sensitive to signs of initiation	sensitive to signs of rejection
may like partner's assertiveness or obvious desire to initiate	may like partner's overt or obvious signs of desire

Fears and Inhibitions:

Activator	*Reflector*
may be codependent, overly concerned about mate's approach, or overly focused on having her desires gratified	may be overly concerned about inability to express bottled-up needs or obtain gratification of his desires
may find it difficult to be aware of her own, very private, "independent from mate" feelings, which can promote more a free, liberated experience	may find it difficult to articulate relationship-orientated feelings, appearing awkward, indecisive, inwardly sheltering—needs to risk a totally passionate experience
deeply fears sense of loneliness and/or exclusion from world of mate (this depletes her sexual energy and desire)	deeply fears sense of confusion or demands from world of mate (this depletes his sexual energy)

Developmental Opportunities for an Activator

Development of Attending Eros

"Be still and know that I am God" is a great promise for activators!

If you are an activator, you may score low on tests of acute observation or present attention skills because you are going too fast! You like having a lot of things on your plate—perhaps too many things to take the time for reflective observation! Appreciating the Sabbath concept of rest is hard for you. You are easily tempted to discount the joy of reflection and "catching up with" your inner person because you obtain energy by doing things.

Yet sexual experience affords you a beautiful opportunity to rediscover your self—the inner person who gets lost in the whirl. You can come home and attend to your neglected side, listening to "messages from base." These are the inner longings you can't or don't hear in the din of noisy daily activity.

I call this ability to focus on your neglected inner person the capacity for *attending eros*. It is experienced in the power of pause.

How to Practice the "Power of Pause"

Did you ever sit and watch a campfire flicker in the wilderness? When I backpack into the High Sierra, I sit by the fire at night and find myself mesmerized by the dancing flame. I watch it cast its light on the rocks and the inky darkness lurking around the campsite. I sink into this strange interplay of dark and light, warm and cold, security and fear. I allow myself to sense if they have a resonance within me, and, indeed, these feelings and themes are present in me, in varying degrees. Yet, a lot of the time, I don't even know it because I'm in too big of a hurry.

The pause by the campfire offers me opportunity to feel tired muscles, soothe them, and help them recuperate. For you activators at home, the power of pause means feeling the losses and gains of the daily battle, and paying deeper attention to your wounds and aches, your joys and triumphs.

In the sexual experience, the "power of pause" means reconnection to the previous joy of companionship that is lost during the day as each lover walks his or her separate pathway. Lying beside your lover, give yourself permission to become more attentive to your longings or quiet things you have been missing in your busy schedule.

> To develop attending eros means to be still and listen to quiet things...like heartbeats (his and yours)...and breathing (his and yours)...and become conscious of the passage of time...the special feel of comfortable time spent together...the short time left to enjoy life and one another.

Of course, these are just small things to a very busy person, isn't that right, Ms. Activator? Wrong! Pause and allow yourself to be moved by the *importance* of these quiet things...the most *important* things in life itself! In these all-too-easily overlooked special moments, you will find the honing mechanism sorely needed to still the bouncing compass needle of your sometimes frazzled soul.

To practice the "power of periodic pause" with your partner is a great way to center yourself and develop greater capacity for *attending eros.*

Developmental Opportunities for the Reflector

Development of Empathetic Eros

If you are a reflector, you tend to live from the inside out. That is, you start from a position of first finding an inner comfort level, and once that is achieved, you move on to considering mutual gratification. This seeking of inner security and self-protection can become a problem if you are shy or awkward in expressing your sexual needs—such as preferences for your own gratification, or a keen desire to learn the preferences of your partner. When it comes to a mutually intimate sexual experience, your partner may wonder "where you are" at times due to your inwardness or tentativeness.

Your mate may not understand that you are readying yourself to find the necessary motivation and energy necessary for a comfortable sexual experience—that is, one that does not position you as vulnerable to rejection. While your tendency to first look within for motivational comfort may feel natural to you, your mate may perceive it as self-centered pleasure seeking. Empathy forces you out of yourself and into the foreign world of relationship-centered feelings, where her drives and needs are of equal power and value to your own.

I call this *empathetic eros.* To make it happen, you must choose to set aside your spectator mode of safe reflection. Instead, you must opt for the courageous action of jumping full-fledged into the sensitive arena required of a mutual experience: possible failure or rejection. Some therapists call this process the calling forth of your inner "warrior," that part of yourself that must be confronted in order to "give yourself away" to some dangerous cause or battle.

For reflectors, being a warrior can take many forms.

For example, I give my wife permission to be demanding and hold me accountable in certain areas. Often these are areas where courageous action is required, and, knowing my reflector tendencies, I would prefer to wait until I feel a little more comfortable before I move ahead. In sexual relations, I want to be an empathetic warrior, meaning being the best lover I can be *for her sake*. This necessitates taking the risk of sincerely asking what things I can do or change in order to please her—sexually or emotionally.

Such questions are not easy to ask. They bring to the surface the potential pain—and gain—of *empathetic eros*. It means saying good-bye to the safety of reflective spectating and hello to the possible wounds of being a warrior in the arena of criticism or guilt. To embrace the role of initiator, whether emotionally or sexually, is to open oneself to the risk side of empathy.

But that's precisely where reflectors need to develop…the realm of *empathetic eros*.

The Planner and the Journeyer

Planner	*Journeyer*
automatic thinking pattern in attitudes toward sex	automatic thinking pattern in attitudes toward sex
(assumed to be male for purpose of illustration only; can be either gender)	(assumed to be female for purpose of illustration only; can be either gender)
prefers sense of order: for example, "rightness" of time and place, morality, surrounding circumstances	Prefers sense of spontaneity: for example, "chemistry" of time and place, prefers a relationship "magic" to move her
forethought, procedures, and rituals are most comfortable precursors	surprises, instant responses, and excitement are preferred to provide "the right spark"
prefers sex that is within limits of control, with the predetermined confines of expectations or routines	prefers sex that has variety, and may push boundaries beyond routine ritual or rules that box-in spontaneity
may be so goal oriented that complete focus is on climax and ignores other aspects of the process	may be so nongoal oriented that complete focus is on freedom to experience the process, and the issue of climax may be secondary
may appear so bound by goal orientation that mutual pleasuring appears forgotten at times	may appear so spontaneous or frivolous that mutual pleasuring appears forgotten at times

Fears or Inhibitions:

Planner	*Journeyer*
may approach sex as a pleasure that first must be "earned" before it can be enjoyed—may be poor "receiver" of gift of pleasure, hence struggle with relaxation	may approach sex as a pleasure that is to be enjoyed only when in the mood—may be poor "giver" when the right feeling is missing, and therefore appear cold or disinterested
may be uncomfortable with sex becoming extremely "wild" physically or extremely emotional	may be uncomfortable with sex becoming extremely "routine" with a physical or emotionally programmed protocol by partner

Opportunity for Development for a Planner

Development of Graceful Eros

The planner is often a poor receiver of gifts, including the gift of unearned joy. Sexual pleasuring throws planners into the rare mode of being a receiver as well as giver. It requires the capacity to open oneself to the goodness of life with its inherent gifts and pleasures that are provided, not only by hard planning and work, but also by gracious providence. For the fore-thinking planner, it feels very bizarre and surprising to experience a gift of joy from another coming purely as a result of unmerited favor, of grace. The gift feels like an unacceptable coloring "outside of the lines" to you because of your natural orientation toward being *responsible* for planning, performing, and giving.

Even more strangely, sometimes you don't even have to initiate anything in the sexual realm: it just sort of happens to you! At times like this, you must deepen your ability to let yourself "go with the flow." It is an unusual but glorious feeling. Give yourself permission to feel the luxury of being seduced by an unstoppable force out to pleasure you. Serendipity is great: it reminds us that we are not in charge of everything! When you permit yourself to "go with the flow," you are developing a greater capacity for *graceful eros!*

As a planner myself, I must admit that in sexuality I am often like the elder brother in the parable of the prodigal son. I have a hard time going to a party that is a spontaneous celebration or a rather dubious, questionable occasion for gathering to have fun. How can you allow yourself to experience great joy at an event with such a problematic basis?

In sexual pleasuring, that "problem" can be my own mind-set that says, "I haven't earned this, or I don't deserve quite this much pleasure." My nature is to be cautious about letting the hedonistic, pleasure side of myself fully experience "the party" of lovemaking. The tight-jawed Puritan work ethic (note: it's not in the Bible!) usurps the Grand Designer's position as sovereign over everything, including the occasional extravagant, serendipitous blessings of sexual pleasure.

How does one practically develop *graceful eros?*

Learn to Play and Discover Joy!

Play is one vehicle through which you can learn to live by grace.

Play is a way of being in the world that forms an individual's own style or art of living. The smart planner understands this and seeks to make it an integral part of his approach to the world. Actually, play is evidence of robust health, both spiritually and psychologically—at any stage of development!

Nevertheless, we planners typically feel guilty when we relax and play. In our driven lifestyles, we easily lose our playful capacity that can counterbalance our natural bent for single-focused or serious-minded living. But lighthearted play is appropriate in sexual relating, and can come in various forms, such as foreplay or sexual bantering.

In the biblical story of Mary and Martha, Jesus gently chides the busyness-oriented Martha by saying, "Mary has chosen the better part." It seems that Martha was skilled at "doing" and Mary was better at "being." Many of us in the production-oriented Western world have taken on the main characteristic of planners, that is, of being better at "doing" than "being." Only in the "being state" can we be fully open to play. It can be an act of faith, showing that we are, indeed, aware and grateful recipients of the gift of life.

How good are you at just "being"? Put differently, how easy is it for you to be consciously aware of your existence as a human being that delights in yourself for no other reason than the fact that, by the grace of God, you are alive. Your sexual highs prove just how alive you can consciously "be"!

By being more sexually spontaneous, we break through into areas of pleasure hidden behind the curtains of constant productivity. By being playful, we get closer to our Maker and His more satisfying, "beyond productivity" purposes and start to deeply enjoy some of His other graces, not the least of which is mutual sexual pleasuring. What vast potential it holds for the tentative elder-son-like planner, who doesn't really know whether or not he is invited—or really wants to come—to the party!

If he doesn't come to the party soon, the party will be over...and with its passing, the opportunity to receive and enjoy deeper levels of *graceful eros* will be lost forever!

Developmental Opportunities for the Journeyer

Development of "Soul-Mating" Eros

The spontaneity-loving journeyer may need a greater appreciation for the kind of intimacy that is privy only to persons married to an opposite. Sex is not just for the moment, a temporary and passing experience. It can be an open gate to your partner's soul. Instead of a pleasing but surface-level experience, sex can be a "soul-mating" adventure that deepens the journeyer by strengthening and enriching her steadfast, total commitment and interest in her mate. In a long-term relationship, this applies particularly to knowing your soul mate—and being known by your soul mate—at deeper and deeper levels. The benefit of this process is the reward of what I call *"soul-mating" eros.*

How do you make this deepening partnership happen?

The "Soul-Mating" Process

To enjoy the pleasures of being in a soul-mate relationship, both parties need to commit to the "soul-mating" process. The first axiom of this process is: in order to find your soul mate, first *you* must become a soul. In this context, I define a soul as a person committed to be a genuine, authentic person, without pretense or superficiality. To be real, like the toy bunny in *The Velveteen Rabbit,* means a willingness to get worn, tossed around, and dirty. For journeyers, that means a readiness to embrace life's necessities, which includes dialogue with one's partner about gritty, disciplined goal setting for the future—including the relationship.

This type of partnering is not the forte of the journeyer, yet goal setting is mandatory, even in relationships. Just as the planner must learn the value of play in the context of lovemaking, so the journeyer must learn the value of being a partner in the ongoing development of her mate. Getting to know him must go deeper than his surface level expressions. It should include knowing his long-term dreams and present angst in fighting the enemies of his progress. His goals need to become your goals as well, so that you can be his empowering advocate and coach.

This applies not only to his professional and long-term life goals, but also his need for personality development in which he needs your help. In all of these goals, he needs the discipline of a coach who comes alongside and holds him (and herself as well) accountable. For many journeyers, the long-term value of a loving, prodding coach goes underappreciated.

How can you get started in this process? Read this section with your mate and talk about it. Consider some of the following:

1. Ask where your mate could use some support, feedback, or developmental coaching...from the one who adores him.

2. Do *you* have goals to develop a new discipline or new skill in the next two years? Are there some parts of yourself that you need to develop, and perhaps could if you asked him to be your gentle "accountability partner"?

3. Have you put off working to improve in some area (perhaps conversations about sex) that could enhance your intimacy or enjoyment?

"To find your soul mate, first be a soul," means that the journeyer must come to value the rewards of his genuineness before, during, or after lovemaking. This is one of the times when is he most "alive," most real, like *The Velveteen Rabbit*. Take advantage of his openness, as this is your chance to know him better! Assume that there are depths to him that lay unexplored, but that he will reveal them when totally relaxed in those raw, private moments of openness to a soul mate. Make it your disciplined goal to listen during these peak moments, sensing how you could become a closer, more caring partner for him, enhancing both of your lives.

This is the development in the realm of *"soul-mating" eros.*

CONCLUSION

The mystery of sexual difference—and personality difference—await greater exploration. In the meantime, I hope the models offered throughout this book have offered new vistas of your "mysterious other." The original glow of promise that emanated from our partners can flicker when the inevitable winds of opposition blow. Having read this book, may those winds be transformed into a constant trade wind of intrigue and challenge, making your relationship ever fresh and profoundly rich as the years pass.

Appendix A

THE BIRTHPLACE OF PERSONALITY

HOW IS PERSONALITY FORMED?

At birth every person is born with unique natural abilities. In this book, I have considered these abilities in the broadest sense as personal capacities or "powers" to get things done. Personality theorists have described them in many ways. The ancient Greeks mistakenly believed they were attributed to the predomination of one's bodily "humors" or fluids, labeling personality according to four categories: melancholic (depressed), sanguine (cheerful), phlegmatic (unemotional), or choleric (irritable).

The Developmental Explanation

The developmental explanation is that our personality approach can be likened to a person developing his right or left hand—inevitably and unconsciously, one of the two becomes the preferred hand. In the same way, after long use, our given personality type becomes our preferred approach. For a right-handed person, the right hand becomes more deft and effective than our left hand, not because the left hand is lacking in ability, but because of repetitive use.

In an unconscious way, our personality preference for certain manners of thinking evolves into what cognitive-behavioral therapists call "automatic thinking." We learn to approach situations in ways that have worked for us in the past. With repetitive use, these lines of thinking become automatic.

To carry the hand analogy a little farther, while we acknowledge the latent ability existing in our left hand, we soon come to unconsciously and automatically *believe* that the right hand is best. It is a bias born of a proven effectiveness than seems to confirm this belief. "Hey, it works," we say. "Isn't that proof that my approach is the best?"

The Theories of Allport and Jung

In more modern times, psychologists such as Allport statistically correlated behaviors and called them "personality traits," such as extraversion.

A giant theorist in the field of personality was the Swiss thinker Carl Jung. His theory is based on the assumption that human motivation is not due to chance, but upon the logical result of observable differences seen in the prevalence of certain diametric types or archetypes.[1] For Jung, the most basic human functional differences sprang from perception and judging. That is, perception starts the process as we first become aware of things, and then we make judgments and conclusions about what has been perceived. He defined all perception as falling into two categories or archetypes on a continuum moving from sensing at one end to intuition on the other. Sensing is a perceptional awareness gained through using the five senses. Intuition is the incorporation of associations with outside stimulus tacked on by the unconscious. It includes everything from hunches to shining achievements of creative art or scientific discovery.[2]

Jung's view differed from Allport's in defining our characteristic orientation toward the world as either extroversion or introversion. Jung believed it to be an issue of perception, whereas Allport considered these traits to be inevitably manifest in social settings. For Jung, the extrovert's interest is most comfortably focused on the outer world of people and things. The introvert's perceptual interest is most comfortably focused on the inner world of ideas and self. Asking each to focus their attention toward their unnatural, uncomfortable sphere of perception results in an eventual energy drain. Interested in the origins and management of psychic energy, Jung was fascinated with the inner-world spark of extroverts and introverts. He was probably a reflective introvert himself.[3]

THE HISTORICAL ROLE OF THE MYERS-BRIGGS TYPE INDICATOR

The need for Jung's theories to become more empirically verifiable became the challenge for Katherine Briggs and daughter Isabel Myers.

Katherine was fascinated by Jung's theories of types, and began to explore and expand them. Isabel became determined to put these theories into practice through the idea of developing a "type indicator." The Myers-Briggs Type Indicator (MBTI) evolved from test results of more than 5,000 medical students and 10,000 nurses in the 1950s. In 1975, the Center for the Application of Psychological Type was organized as a service and ongoing research laboratory for the Indicator. By the late 1970s, the MBTI had become the most widely used personality measure for nonpsychiatric populations. Today, it is widely accepted as the leading instrument in the field of personality analysis.[4]

PERSONALITY EXPRESSION THROUGH MOTIVATIONAL OR SPIRITUAL GIFTS

In spiritual work, we refer to certain personal gifts as "spiritual gifts" or special "graces." Taken from the Greek word *charis* meaning charismatic, these graces are powers or capacities to do things with an extraordinary ease or deft ability. We sometimes refer to capable persons as "charismatic" individuals in recognizing a special personal endowment or genius to do something well. In some circles, they are called "motivational gifts," the assumption being that a Higher Power has innately imbued persons with a deep or mysterious motivation that results in a functionality or vocation uniquely meant for them. This definition explains a natural inclination to be motivated in certain ways of functioning that transcends a strictly psychological explanation.

THE MYSTERY OF OPPOSITE TYPES AND MARRIAGE

"Integrationists" have proposed that an intersection of Jungian psychology and Judeo-Christian theology can be found in the primal urge to marry an opposite. This is the complementary concept, or the notion that mates are consciously or subconsciously aware that a piece of their potential for wholeness is missing. Marriage to an opposite fulfills this primal, profound longing. It is what Jung might call "wholeness" and theologians might call a master plan for "completion" or "providence." (Cf. Genesis 2, *"it is not good for man to be alone ... I will make a helper for him."*) For more on the complementary concept, I refer readers to Harville Hendricks, *How to Get the Love You Want* (Henry Holt and Company, New York, N.Y., 1988).

This view is in concert with humanistic psychology, springing from the human potential school that posits personality as an evolving construct. From this perspective, every personality has within it a potential for wholeness and fulfillment in a way analogous to the potential of all humanity itself evolving toward greater fulfillment.

Consider the farmer who has developed only 70 acres of the 100 he owns. He has previously viewed the last 30 acres as being somewhat inferior, but decides one year to develop the entire 100 acres. No matter what happens, he can now consider himself a "whole" farmer. Why? Whether or not the land turns out to be fertile, he has sought to develop every possible potentiality granted to him.

In the same way, I believe there are latent capacities in the shadowy personality of each of us that are waiting to be called forth. Why not think of getting married to an opposite as one of the most beautiful ways to tease them out? But we must be committed to becoming fully developed, to being a real or "whole" person—even if it comes through exploration of fear-provoking areas of discomfort in our relationship. I hope this book brings light to these shadowy areas that will invite more exploration.

Appendix B

CHANGING THE MOOD
OF A MARRIAGE

THE HALF BLINDNESS INHERENT IN
PERSONALITY PREFERENCE

When conflict inevitably arises due to personality differences, our usual "automatic thinking" has a tendency to close us off to other approaches. Our belief about what is a functional approach to a problem is far narrower than we think. In marriage, while not always verbalized so bluntly, it often goes like this: "My approach is 'superior' to yours. You just don't understand that (which, indeed, could be more evidence that I see things better than you do!)."

The fallacy of this very natural misbelief is aptly illustrated in the tale of the proverbial blind couple who grab hold of an elephant. He grabs the tail and exclaims, "An elephant is a skinny creature!" She grabs the leg and exclaims, "An elephant is a stocky creature!"

Both are half blind! Neither party sees the entire picture. They don't see or sense significant dimensions of reality—until they get input from the other. Our personality preferences, though they work quite well for us most of the time, also have the downside of rendering us "blind" to the effectiveness of other approaches. There is a reward for those who will take a longer look, for it is at the point of difference that true love (not courtship love) is formed in the crucible of choices to follow the higher— and, yes, the harder—road.

The humbling and momentous question constantly raised by the marriage bond is this: Can you entertain the idea that what you have previously deemed to be the whole picture is merely a portion?

Now, let me get even closer to home. Is it possible that my preferred approach, while it may work effectively for me, might be equaled or surpassed by what I have previously written off as Helen's "inferior" approach?

Reality dictates that in a long-term relationship, the following misbelief be completely banished from your mind-set:

My level of marital satisfaction depends primarily upon my partner.

All too often in marriage therapy, I see two partners overfocused on the challenges of their grating differences, as if to say, "If only the other would change, then I would be happy." Get this straight, friends: Personality types are established for life! They cannot be changed, except by asking a person to forfeit his or her own integrity of personality. (We should never ask anyone to corrupt their personhood, the individual and unique soul that they were created to be.) *Absolutely forget* the notion of changing the personality of your mate in any way!

THE OFTEN UNSPOKEN BUT DISTURBING QUESTION

We are so different that sometimes I ask, "Will I ever find the satisfaction I hoped for in my marriage?"

This fear is raised when differences grate at the passion of earlier years. I use the term "passion" not as in the fabricated Hollywood version, but in the sense of a "liking to be with" feeling, a pleasant attraction that desires to partner with and be a partner to another. This feeling is without reservation, regret, or wistful thoughts of desiring to be with another. The largest passion drainers are differing life values, temperament, and personality types. I touch only briefly on life values (belief systems) and slightly on temperament (decision making). Psychology can offer no cure for radically different values (e.g., glaring character flaws that remain unaddressed). Moreover, personality pathology as found in psychological disorders are outside the bounds of this book. I have assumed that your opposite is not neurotic. If he or she is, see a licensed, experienced marriage therapist now!

However, I have good news when it comes to differences of personality type! They can be converted from passion-draining to passion-sustaining. The key is a "deeper-than-courtship" understanding of the differences. Promise comes through the new revolution in psychology—cognitive behavioral therapy. In this case, its tools are applied specifically to marriage.

For example, do you want to change your feelings about your mate? It's a simple process, but not easy. Here's how both psychology and theology say it works: Change your thoughts about your partner and you will change your feelings about your partner.

But how can you change your thoughts?

CHANGING HOW YOU FEEL TOWARD YOUR MATE

In marriage, we are most often motivated by our positive or negative beliefs about one another. The cognitive revolution has restored the mind-mood connection, which postulates that our attitudes (mind) are the key determinates of feelings (mood). If the filter of our mind (see chapter 3) believes an event to be positive, then we will have corresponding feelings such as joy or pleasure. Conversely, if our mind interprets an event to be negative, there will be an inevitable connection with "downer" feelings that follow.

In other words, thoughts precede feelings. While the thoughts may be automatic, they nevertheless become the critical tool to alter mood states, which are vital in a satisfying marriage. If you have reached the point where you no longer believe or trust in the promise of your opposite, satisfaction is virtually doomed. You must find reason to believe again. But, where do you find such a reason to believe when obvious discouragement or an underlying despair is slowly eating away the relationship?

Discover the hidden gold in your personality differences! Are your differences real? Yes. Are they exciting? No! That's because of your half blindness! The treasures have been hidden—up until now!

Appendix C

TWO ABSOLUTES ABOUT MARITAL SATISFACTION

ABSOLUTE NUMBER 1

Respect the integrity of the other's personality.

Marriage satisfaction is essentially based upon the difficult decision to (1) *respect* and (2) *appreciate* someone whose approaches to life are, at the minimum, partially different than your own[1] or, at the maximum, different in every category![2] After reading the previous chapters you may have observed that you are opposites in every section. Don't despair, my wife and I are opposites, too—and we have learned to love it!

In almost half of the marriages today, to *respect* and *appreciate* differences calls for a level of personal growth that is too much for one or both. Citing "irreconcilable differences," they end in divorce.

It does not have to be so!

I wrote this book to make the pivotal choice to *respect* and *appreciate* our different other more compelling, more intriguing, and more fascinating. It works, because it is at the heart of love!

Where Love Grows or Dies: At the Point of Difference

It is at our point of difference that we choose to follow one of two roads. The first is the high road: to somehow find the ability to *respect* the other.

The second is the low road: to choose contempt or rejection. To label another as inferior, foolish, or simply strange is a momentous choice, for it pours cold water upon the bonfire of hope for continuing passion within the relationship. Yet, incredibly, the reactive pathway of contempt is the one that many select! They make the common mistake of accepting societal wisdom, such as, "enmity between the sexes is inevitable and irredeemable." Neither psychology nor theology believe that—so don't buy into it yourself!

Believe that personality differences are there, not to frustrate you, but to fulfill you. *There is no getting around the necessity for respect in order for this to happen!*

ABSOLUTE NUMBER 2

Learn to appreciate your different mate.

I use the word *appreciate* in the deepest sense. Jesus appreciated the gift of life itself. He appreciated bread (God is so great, He gives small pleasures as well as big ones!). Jesus appreciated the beauty of the lilies of the field. He appreciated every living human being as sacred, as a "gift."

When a marriage partner ceases to find something in his or her partner as a gift to appreciate in this sense of humble gratitude, a cancer on the relationship is born. Before long, the basic psychological reason to be married, to enhance your experience of life, is called into question. In today's society, altruistic reasons for staying married (for the children's sake, for career, for parents, etc.) are no longer sufficient to maintain an emotionally malnourishing relationship. In today's culture, as many leery young people can attest, being single can hold more promise to enhance one's life than a mundane marriage. Unless there is a means of emotional replenishment *within* a relationship, the demands of *giving* to it will eventually burn it out.

So, the following critical questions are raised: How do I come to appreciate someone who is so mysterious to me? How can this person who is so different enhance my life?

The Emotional Problem with Differences:
Confronting Fear of Change

Early in life we are taught to fear strangers. It stays with us as a lurking, subconscious prejudice toward the different, the foreign, and the strange. Fear leads us down the self-protective pathway of safety, routine, and comfort. We become self-centered creatures of habit, robots of the routine. If we allow this orientation of self-comfort to become our central psychological orientation toward different others, we can become dulled in the boredom of our psychic ruts.

Perhaps the dulling effect of our psychic ruts is best illustrated in Kirkegaard's dream about heaven and hell. As he visited hell, he noticed the anguished longing of people gathered around a large banquet table filled with bounteous food. As he drew closer, he noted that the frustrated citizens of hell were trying to eat, but couldn't. They were seated around the table with handcuffs fastened to a long rod. Each person would take the food in his spoon and try to feed himself, consequently throwing the others off. Each stubbornly stuck to his own routine, doing it solely his way, oblivious to the notion that there might be a different approach that could work better.

Then Kirkegaard visited heaven, where he noted the same sumptuous banquet table loaded with appetizing delights. Here, the citizens seemed so happy, though they also were chained together. As he drew closer, he discovered the reason. Each person was delightfully exploring new ways, not to feed himself, but to feed others at the table. Far from feeling entrapped in their own frustrating, routine way of doing things, they were delighting in the exploration of new avenues of feeding others. In the process, they ended up being wonderfully fed themselves!

This is the blessing and curse of our own personality preferences! We subconsciously come to rely upon our safe and routine approach to the world as if it is exclusive or superior. Good news: illumination is not far away!

Moving toward Trust in the Unseen

An essential element of appreciation in a love relationship is trust. Trust is the process of letting go, of detachment from control, of choosing faith rather than fear. It is a portal to a more abundant, ever-expanding life. It is this ability in a relationship to cross over the threshold from self-defending paralysis to growth that defines our spiritual character and marital maturity.

Trust lifts us above the animal-like survival instinct of primal fear. Its momentous importance as a gateway to spiritual wholeness is confirmed in virtually every great religion, from Christianity to Zen Buddhism. "If you have faith...you can say to this mountain, 'Move,' and it will be done," Jesus promised his disciples (Mt. 21:21). Yet, it is so difficult to trust: Where are the dimensions of new life yet to be learned from another whom I believe I know so well?

Learning to trust more starts with a yearning to trust more—to be a more trusting person, open to the newness of life. You start by admitting your own spiritual poverty, your tendency to take the easy road of fear or disdain of the unfamiliar. If you acknowledge your rutted road of a particular fear, it becomes, in itself, a beacon to the specific threshold of possibility for new growth. All spiritual growth starts with where you are, not where you want to be. Alas, there is no detour around the reality that some degree of discomfort lies ahead because it means saying good-bye to the comfortable road of holding on and staying put in your current doubt. Nevertheless, it is the pathway to self-discovery.

To illustrate, I will relate my personal journey from acute stage fright to relative relaxation in public speaking. As a reflector type (see chapter 5), I was introverted, and found energy in observing life as much as in actively participating in it. In high school, I regarded taking speech and drama class as a trip to hell itself! Sitting out in the audience of life, God called me into the ministry. By so doing, I would have to step up to the speaker's platform every Sunday morning and face my fears. On Saturday nights, I would lie in bed with a churning stomach, and dream of losing preaching notes minutes before I was to speak. In my frequent nightmare, I would stand in front of the congregation and stare at them in humiliating silence, with nothing to say, paralyzed by fear and displaying my performance anxiety to all.

This calling to move from the comfortable preferred dimension of being a reflector to the new dimension of an activator was precisely where God wanted me to be! Like many married partners, I felt like I was forced into a situation where all I could do was *trust*—or bail out! As the years went by, I found myself even growing excited about preaching, needing fewer and fewer notes, as a statement of my own ability to exercise trust. I finally reached the day when I took the big leap and spoke without a single note!

I discovered something in the process about my own blindness. I needed to grow in several ways. I had considered myself a fairly confident person, but now I was in a situation where my lack of self-confidence was being sorely tested—in order for it to grow. I was reticent by nature to try new experiences, and now I was fully "out there," exploring a new frontier of being. I was connecting in a profound way to the outward world of people and things as I looked into people's faces from the pulpit. My mind moved from attention on myself to attentiveness to their conditions and needs. I found myself more fully participating in life rather than living as a spectator. I found myself expanding, becoming more alive and aware, more passionately involved in this wide and wonderful world.

God had moved me across the threshold, for a time, from my preferred perspective of the reflector dimension to the new world of the activator. There is a saying that "once a mind has been expanded, it never returns to its old shape." I would amend this statement to say, "Once a threshold has been effectively crossed, your world is never the same again!"

The Energy to Cross Over to a New Dimension

How does a relationship that evolves over a period of time remain alive and dynamic?

A marriage with an opposite holds great potential because relationships are renewed by the constant challenge and promise of self-expansion! Self-expansion leads to the discovery of new realms of reality, new experiences of ever-expanding awareness of the wonders present in this world. These wonders are waiting for us to discover them, but we cannot get there alone. Remember, "It is not good for man to be alone," (The Holy Bible, Genesis 2:18). Long after the biological and sociological explanations of the "urge to merge" are satisfied, there remains a deeper mystery. Was this particular, strange person really meant for me—selected by a yearning that holds within its specific urges a higher wisdom?

Yes, for this yearning springs from within our unconscious inner being, not solely from the more conscious attraction of our opposite during courtship. Our need to move toward wholeness was subconsciously fueling our attraction. This is why the patience required to maintain respect and appreciation for your other is so important: In the long run, you will begin to take on some of the characteristics of our opposite, the very characteristics that may identify some of the unconscious, empty spaces that God wants to fill!

CONCLUSION: A NEW ADVENTURE

In marriage therapy, the crisis of marital distress is often a failure to believe that I, not my partner, am the problem. Why am I the problem? Because I admit no energy to expand or be open to change required by a deeper exploration of my mate's approach. I urge a new attitude, as expressed so beautifully by a lady who I visited when I was serving as a pastor. She was in her late eighties, and had just a few weeks to live. She had the refreshing capacity, as do many elderly, to be completely candid. I asked her if she had any regrets as she looked back over her life.

She replied, "Oh yes, Pastor Ron, I have a few. My parents taught me to be the careful type, but I would take more chances if I could live my life over again. I would take more little adventures. Though I didn't do it, I always wanted to take more exploratory Sunday afternoon rides to different places. You know, to get out of the boring ruts I could so easily fall into. What I'm saying is that I see now that the cautious life was more my own fear than God's way."

This book is about more explorative Sunday afternoon rides beckoning with the promise of finding hidden treasure in a strange new land. If you are willing to go exploring on a new adventure, there are some surprising Sunday afternoon vistas ahead for you—right in your own neighborhood—from your opposite personality type!

NOTES

CHAPTER 1: WHY OPPOSITES *ARE* MEANT FOR EACH OTHER

1. Isabel Briggs Myers with Peter B. Myers, *Gifts Differing* (Palo Alto, Calif.: Consulting Psychologists Press, Inc., 1980), 128.

2. Daniel Goleman, *Emotional Intelligence: Why It Can Matter More than Intelligence* (London: Bloomsbury Publishing, 1996), 96.

3. Yuichi Shoda, Walter Mischel, and Phillip Peake, "Predicting Adolescent Cognitive and Self-Regulatory Competencies from the Preschool Delay of Gratification," *Developmental Psychology* 26, no. 6 (1990): 978–86.

4. Goleman, *Emotional Intelligence,* 143.

5. John Gottman, *What Predicts Divorce: The Relationship between Marital Processes and Marital Outcomes* (Hillsdale, N.J.: Lawrence Erlbaum Associates, Inc., 1993).

6. Ibid.

CHAPTER 2: DECISION MAKING: THE FEELER VS. THINKER COLLISION

1. John Gottman, *What Predicts Divorce: The Relationship between Marital Processes and Marital Outcomes* (Hillsdale, N.J.: Lawrence Erlbaum Associates, Inc., 1993).

2. Ibid., 119–20.

3. Ted L. Huston, Principal Researcher, "Behavioral Buffers on the Effects of Negativity on Marital Satisfaction," Abstract, the PAIR Project (Austin: University of Texas at Austin, 1994).

4. Daniel Goleman, *Emotional Intelligence: Why It Can Matter More than Intelligence* (London: Bloomsbury Publishing, 1996), 40.

5. Ted L. Huston, Principal Researcher, "Courtship Antecedents of Marital Satisfaction and Love," Abstract, the PAIR Project (Austin: University of Texas at Austin, 1994).

6. Goleman, *Emotional Intelligence*, 85.

7. Ibid., 80.

APPENDIX A: THE BIRTHPLACE OF PERSONALITY

1. C. G. Jung, *Psychological Types* (New York: Harcort Brace, 1923).

2. J. Jacobi, *The Psychology of C. G. Jung* (New Haven, Conn.: Yale University Press, 1968).

3. Isabel Briggs Myers, *Gifts Differing* (Palo Alto, Calif.: Consulting Psychologists Press, Inc. 1980).

4. Ibid.

APPENDIX C: TWO ABSOLUTES ABOUT MARITAL SATISFACTION

1. In unpublished research, Isabel Myers found in 375 couples that 44 percent had three or four out of the four possible categories in common. In other words, 56 percent had one or more personality categories that were not in common. Only 4 percent had none of the four categories in common, as do the author and his wife.

2. In a recent study of 426 couples, Nancy S. Marioles found that it is "more likely that people be attracted to and marry someone of the same type than they are a person of the opposite type." She found women were dissatisfied 33 percent and 31 percent of the time when married to an INTP (Introversion, Intuition, Thinking, Perceptive) or an INFS (Introversion, Intuition, Feeling, Sensing), respectively. These Myers-Briggs categories would most closely correspond to my designation of a reflector and envisioner type: the man who prefers his inner world of thought and feeling, as well as viewing the world as full of possibilities and visions. One possibility is that, for this type of men, it may take more work to enter their inner world and understand it than for other types.

RECOMMENDED READING LIST FOR COUPLES

Reaching Out: The Three Movements of the Spiritual Life, by Henri J.M. Nouwen.

> The opening section on the value of solitude and self-awareness as a starting place for spiritual health is one of the best I have read over the years. Excellent for extroverts who just don't get the importance of periodic introversion, reflection, and self-awareness vis-à-vis a surface-level conformity to the immediate world around them.

Reinventing Your Life: How to Break Free from Negative Life Patterns, by Jeffery Young and Janet Klosko.

> Excellent for those who had a broken or dysfunctional start in their psychological development as a result of poor or abusive parenting.

The Road Less Traveled, by M. Scott Peck.

> Chapter 1 is Peck's classic work on the importance of accepting the difficulty of life as a growth opportunity, and delaying gratification (some say the number one skill in emotional intelligence). Section 1 on discipline and section 2 on love are the best parts of this popular classic on psychological health.

The Secret of Staying in Love, by John Powell.

> A classic on the topic of emotional dialogue, the importance of emotional disclosure, and every emotion as a self-revelation. Great for tin men who minimize the importance in marriage of sharing feelings, of sharing "self," and doing the "work of love" in terms of self-disclosure, which is the pathway to deeper intimacy.Index

INDEX

About the Author

RON SHACKELFORD is a licensed Marriage and Family Therapist in California and has more than 25 years experience counseling couples. He holds a Doctorate of Ministry in Marriage and Family Therapy degree from Fuller Theological Seminary.

The author can be contacted at innerscape@earthlink.net or at his Web site, marriedtoanopposite.com.